THE

HAND-BOOK

OF

HISTORY AND CHRONOLOGY.

EMBRACING

MODERN HISTORY, BOTH EUROPEAN AND AMERICAN,
FOR THE 16TH, 17TH, 18TH, AND 19TH
CENTURIES.

FOR

STUDENTS OF HISTORY,

AND ADAPTED TO ACCOMPANY

THE MAP OF TIME.

By Rev. JOHN M. GREGORY, LL. D.,
Regent of Illinois Industrial University, and late Superintendent of
Public Instruction for the State of Michigan.

CHICAGO:
ADAMS, BLACKMER, AND LYON.
New York: A. S. Barnes & Co.
1867.

COMPOSITION BY
BROWN & COLBERT,
CHICAGO.

CHICAGO TYPE FOUNDRY,
J. CONAHAN,
STEREOTYPER.

INTRODUCTION.

Geography and Chronology have been called the two eyes of History. History must be viewed through both of these, to be seen in its true relations. Through the first we discern the position of events in *space* or *territory;* through the second we discover their position in *time.* Under the light of these two, all historical causes and consequences are discovered.

The succession of events in time, and their contiguity or connection in territory, are the elementary notions of history. These are the visible features of history,—the external relations under which the ideas and inner forces of history reveal themselves. A chapter of events wholly unrelated in time and unconnected in space, is not history, but a mere jumble of separate incidents, having no necessary connections, and no certain historic value.

Definition.

History is, properly, the record of a series of events, so related in *time,* and in *territory,* that we may infer their connection with some common principle or cause, and their association with the life of some individual or community. The doings of individuals and nations constitute a part, but not the whole of history.

Two Conditions of the Study of History.

The two essential conditions to a successful study of history, are, 1st: To learn accurately the *place where* the several events occurred. 2d: To fix in memory the *time when* they occurred.

Without a strict and constant compliance with these conditions, there can be no valuable nor successful study of this great branch of knowledge. It is the common neglect of these that renders the study of history so useless and uninteresting to most students and readers. Whoever will faithfully keep these elements of time and place clearly fixed in mind, will find history grow luminous before him, and to him it will rise in interest, from the mere recital of an uncertain story, to the almost visible movement of great nations, and of celebrated characters and events.

The First Condition.

The first of these conditions,—the determining of the *place* of events,—is to be met only by a constant reference to good maps. The student or reader of history should never permit himself to go forward with the story without pausing to look up, on the map, with the aid of a good Gazetteer, if necessary, the place of every event mentioned; to trace the course of every march or migration; and to fix in mind every change in territory or boundaries. It may be added, there can be no more profitable study of Geography than this which associates the various localities by their historical connections. Dr. Arnold not only strongly asserts the importance of Geography to History, but insists that the only proper way to study geography is in connection with history.

The Second Condition.

The second condition,—the learning of the *time* of events,—is met by the use of "The Map of Time." This Chart of History and Chronology, assuming space, rather than numbers, as a symbol of time, presents the field of historic time to the eye, in such clear and definite outline, and in such plainly marked subdivisions, that each century, and each year in the century, is easily distinguished.

A true and complete view of chronology must comprehend three distinct things, viz: 1st, the simple date of each prominent event; 2d, the length of periods between prominent dates; and 3d, the synchronisms of history, or the view of contemporary history. All of these three are presented to the eye, in this chart, in so obvious a way, that they are all learned at once, by the same effort; or rather, the first being studied, the other two are learned of necessity and without effort.

Description of the Chart.

The entire chart is arranged on a system of fives, in accordance with the following simple and fundamental philosophy. The *local association* of ideas, (on which the whole chart is constructed,) while it is easily formed, and of great strength and permanency, is easily confused unless the places to be remembered are somewhat prominent in position, and form natural resting places for the eye. Now, everything that has length, has three such prominent resting places; viz., the two ends and the middle. Between each end and the middle, another point or space may be assumed, distinguishable because it is neither end nor middle. Thus we have five sufficiently marked places for the local association to rest on. Taking this basis, the centuries of the Christian Era are divided into four groups of five centuries each, the last group being not yet full. These groups are arranged as follows:

1	2	3	4	5

6	7	8	9	10

11	12	13	14	15

16	17	18	19	

The chart now offered to the public embraces only the last group of centuries, reaching from the sixteenth to the nineteenth. It covers the era of Modern and of American History.

Each century, as in the following cut, being first divided into half centuries, these are again subdivided into five decades or periods of ten years each. Each decade is then divided into two lines of years, five years in each line; and thus every year has its own fixed and distinct place in the map of the century, so arranged that its date can be read at a glance.

Century I.

1	2	3	4	5
6	7	8	9	10
11	12	13	14	15
16	17	18	19	20
21	22	23	24	25
26	27	28	29	30
31	32	33	34	35
36	37	38	39	40
41	42	43	44	45
46	47	48	49	50
51	52	53	54	55
56	57	58	59	60
61	62	63	64	65
66	67	68	69	70
71	72	73	74	75
76	77	78	79	80
81	82	83	84	85
86	87	88	89	90
91	92	93	94	95
96	97	98	99	100

The century stands forth before the eye with a broad, State-like expanse, while its decades and years lie clearly marked and easily distinguished, like so many counties and townships. It is in no very narrow sense, therefore, a *map* of *time;* and, if properly used, will be found to aid the student and reader of History, as maps of the continents aid the student of Geography.

Only a few events in each nation's history are represented on the map, as it is not designed to fix upon the memory anything but a general outline of Chronology. If this outline is retained, the remainder of the history will easily assume its proper place within it.

The more important events are indicated in large type, and these alone are to be learned at the outset, and to be used in the class drills. Those given in the small type are designed only to aid the student to locate, the more readily, the events learned in his study of the intervening history.

The names of monarchs and rulers are given at the date of their accession to power. The names of eminent scholars, artists, and writers, are in ornamental type, and usually occur in the year of their birth.

The nationalities of the characters and events are indicated by the colors. The English dates are indicated by the red color, either covering the whole type, or drawn in a line beneath; the French, by blue; the Spanish, by yellow; the German, by green, &c. The same colors, placed as a border around the words, are used to indicate other, but usually, connected nationalities. Thus, the Scotch dates are shown by a border of red, the Portuguese by a border of yellow, &c., as explained on the Chart itself. When, as in a war, or league, or peace, two or more nationalities are united in the same event, the colors belonging to the several parties are used, the color of the dominant or victorious nation coming first.

The events of American History are left uncolored, and are placed in the lower part of the year spaces. Some other events not belonging to the history of any one nation alone, are also without color. The dates have been verified with great care, and may be relied on as correct.

METHOD OF USING THE MAP.

The map may be used in connection with any good text-book in American, or general history. It will usually be found better to pursue the study of each nation's history by itself, for a century at least. A lesson may be given out, embracing two or three of the events marked on the map. These events should be learned from this hand-book, and their place carefully observed on the chart. The intervening history may then be studied more fully in the text-book in use. Care must be taken that every town, river, country, &c., mentioned, be searched out, and its position be learned, from some good map.

Instead of learning all the events in the order in which they occur on the chart, it will be found best to take first those in the largest type, and afterwards fill up the outline, by learning those in the smaller type.

At each recitation, the lesson of the previous day should be thoroughly reviewed, and a series of back reviews should be constantly in progress. In these reviews, the chart should be kept in constant use, and every opportunity should be taken to call the attention to the chart, so that its outlines may be thoroughly fastened upon the memory. The success in teaching will be exactly proportioned to the clearness and permanency, with which the chart is impressed on the memory.

The following system of rapid review questions upon the chart, will be found useful. First, let the teacher name successively the dates, as "1509," "1530," "1547," &c., the pupils responding promptly, as each date is named, "Accession of Henry VIII.," "Death of Wolsey," "Accession of Edward VI.," &c., giving the event as found on the chart, for the date mentioned. Whenever several facts are given in any year, on the chart, the pupil may be required to mention the one which belongs to the history of the nation under consideration.

Then, reversing the order, let the teacher call out, "Accession of Henry VIII.," "Cardinal Wolsey, Chancellor," "Battle of Flodden," and the pupils give in reply the dates, "1509," "1515," "1513." In this way the whole chart can be passed in rapid review. During these drills the chart should, of course, be unseen by the pupils.

A third form of drill and review, to be used frequently, is to allow the pupils to commence at the beginning of the chart, or of any century, and describe fully the events as they come in order on the chart, giving more or less of the connecting history, as time permits.

As a fourth and most important form of review, the pupil should be required to reproduce the chart rapidly on the black-board. Each pupil may be assigned a different century, or a different decade in the same century. After several nations have been studied, one pupil may be required to fill in the events of one nationality, a second those of another, and so on. Or one may fill in the wars and battles, another the peaces and leagues, a third the accession of monarchs, &c. Colored crayons should be used when practicable. Each pupil should be able to produce the entire chart with rapidity and correctness.

The pupils should also be encouraged, if not required, to make neat copies of the chart, on suitable paper, to be preserved for reference.

The ingenious teacher will devise other methods of drill, to be conducted by the pupils themselves, such as allowing them to attempt to puzzle each other; or to choose sides, &c., &c.

It will be found a valuable exercise for older classes, to assign frequently to the several pupils topics, as some battle, or league, to be carefully read up in some of the larger and fuller histories or cyclopedias, thus cultivating in them the habit of original investigation. Advantage should be taken of all questions which arise in the class, relating to dates, persons, places, or events, to send the pupils to good authors to gain the answers for themselves. Facts thus learned are retained longer than all others, and he is the best teacher who can awaken the most of this spirit of critical inquiry, and can get from his pupils the most of fresh and original research to answer such inquiries.

A final and very useful exercise is that of writing from memory sketches of assigned portions of the history studied. These sketches may embrace the general history of a period, or the wars of a century, or the reign of a monarch, or the history of some particular peace or war. Perhaps no more efficient method than this, can be devised of teaching the difficult and dreaded art of composition.

The Grades in History.

In History, as in every other branch of learning, there are several planes of knowledge, answering to the successive stages of mental development in the child. Here, as elsewhere, the true teacher will carefully note the grade to which his pupils belong, and adapt his lessons, not only in length, but also in substance, to their mental condition.

The simplest stage of historical knowledge is that of biography,—the doings of historic characters. These doings, with the time and place of their occurrence, the simple reasons and consequences of them, and the obvious good or evil growing out of them, will be found interesting to children in the primary grade of instruction.

The second stage embraces the doings of nations as controlled by the more obvious and practical principles of national life, such as the ambition of rulers, the people's love of liberty, the desire of conquest, or of territory,—wars, battles, sieges, marches, and migrations,—the rise, increase, and decadence of nations,—their civilization, arts, usages, and character; together with the right or wrong of the several actions and the causes and consequences of the various movements.

This stage of historical science will be found to meet precisely the active temper, and the practical turn of judgment and imagination, of the pupils of the middle grade in education; and if the study be pursued, with the practical exercises of chart-making and map-drawing, the study will be full of interest and also of profit to these pupils.

The highest stage or plane of historical science embraces the philosophy of History—the investigation of historical causes, the analysis of historical elements, the higher criticism of historical events, epochs, and ideas, and the final contemplation of historical phenomena as the evolution of great historical, ethical, or ethnological forces. This branch of history belongs to the last and highest grade of scholarship in the schools. Its successful prosecution implies the conquest of the primary and intermediate stages, just as the successful study of the higher mathematics requires the preliminary knowledge and drill of the lower branches.

Suggestions for Private Readers of History.

History, wisely read, is one of the most fruitful sources of knowledge and pleasure. As it is ordinarily read, it simply amuses as a story, and leaves no clear pictures in the memory, nor great truths in the understanding.

There are two prevalent methods pursued in the reading of history, which are almost equally shallow and useless. The first is, what a friend of mine calls, "*vagabondizing* in history,"—reading by snatches, here and there, as time favors and books present themselves, without any system or purpose. The second is the dogged reading of long courses of history, made up of heavy volumes, through which the reader plods, under a sense of duty, and from which he comes more weary than wise, glad that the book is finished, but with a painful sense of having wasted time for nought.

The best method of reading history is analagous to that of painting a picture. The true artist does not go hap-hazard to his canvas, and paint here an eye and there a foot, just as the fancy strikes him, or as his colors may chance to serve, without any plan of the picture to be made, or thought of the relative position of the parts. Nor does he begin at one extremity, as the tip of the finger, and go patiently from part to part as they come in course, finishing each part as he advances. Instead of all this, he first produces on his canvas a sketch, or mere outline, of the proposed picture, determining the position and size of each figure and scene. Then, within this guiding outline, he works as his taste directs, or the light favors, or colors are mixed, or his strength permits. He brings out into clearer light, now a hand, now the brow, now a fold in the drapery, keeping his eye upon the entire piece, and preserving carefully the proportions and agreements of all its parts. He visits again and again, with his brush, each particular feature, and retouches, with increasing delight, till the master piece is done, and each part stands forth distinct, beautiful, and harmonious.

So let the reader, who would transfer to his mind the picture of some great historic period, fix in memory the briefest outline of the chosen period, by noting the events which mark the beginning and end of the period, with a very few of the more prominent, intermediate points. Let him carefully fix the dates of these events, and measure in mind the lapse of intervening times. Let him notice also some chief points of contemporaneous history, and take especial care to find out the general geography of the region where the history transpired. This outline he may wisely go over two or three times, with fuller authorities, till the events begin to connect themselves into a consistent story, keeping carefully in view the *time* and *place* of each new fact he adds to the outline.

After this let him not confine himself to any rigid course, but let him read where the taste, or want of the hour, prompts him. Let him assume more and more the character of the investigator, following out the new historical questions which will constantly arise, and seeking to solve the problems which present themselves; sometimes tracing events upward to their historic causes, sometimes following them downward to their results; now pursuing some question of civilization, or law of politics, or art, to its rise in history, and now searching out some obscure historic allusion; but always, with every effort, keeping in mind the outline, and striving to complete the view of the central period.

The reading should start with this central period; but it will not end there. Long lines of historic facts will gather around, and, just as, when one climbs a mountain, every step upward increases the extent of the outlook over the surrounding country, so every added view of the particular field of study, will give a wider comprehension of related fields, and adjacent periods.

It will be seen that this plan proposes, as its aim, not some general knowledge of universal history, but rather a thorough acquaintance with some special period, or part of history. One of the most glaring faults of the courses of historical reading, often proposed to the young, is that they aim to take the reader over the entire field of history. The absurdity of this is seen in the fact that the author of one of these "courses of reading," given not for professional, but for common readers, remarks that the course will occupy ten years. It is safe to assume that long ere the end is reached, the beginning and middle will be forgotten.

The field of universal history is too vast for the conquest of one lifetime; but he will most nearly reach it who will begin by making some one portion of history thoroughly his own. He will establish thus a base in the territory he would conquer, a maneuver as important in mental as in military conquests. And in the thorough study of one portion, he will gain not only critical insight and power, but increased appetite, for the study of other periods. It is not denied that one may gain such a general view of universal history as to know something of every important period and every leading nation. But this falls far short of that full and familiar knowledge which alone is of practical value.

The wise reader will always take advantage of the special desires for information awakened in his own mind, in the course of his reading,—the sudden questions started by something he reads or hears. We never read so profitably, or with such intense interest, as when we read to satisfy a doubt, or answer our own questions. The knowledge gained in this way is the most permanent and the most productive of all our knowledge. It comes to a mind eager to receive it, and enters at once into the practical beliefs and opinions.

To render knowledge. profitable and permanent, it must be largely mingled with clear and critical thought, and such thought is best attained by writing. Let the reader carefully write out the thoughts which are suggested by his reading, and his reading will become steadily more and more critical and productive.

In accordance with the above plan of reading, we offer to private readers "The Map of Time," as affording just the outline needed as a basis for a profitable study of the modern eras in history, and as presenting that outline so clearly pictured on the fields of time as to give it the highest possible value. The sketches of history in this hand-book will help to improve and complete the outline, while the references to authors and books, under the sketches of events, will furnish the reader valuable hints for a fuller course of reading.

The references to books under each date are given to aid students and private readers in finding fuller accounts of the events described. Only a part of the authorities used in the preparation of the hand-book are given in the references, the object being to require as few authorities as the reader can well get along with. The editions used of the several books referred to are the following :—

Bancroft's History of the United States, 9 Vols., Little, Brown, & Co., Boston.
Lossing's History of the United States, large octavo, Mason Brothers, N. Y.
Irving's Life and Voyages of Columbus, 2 Vols., G. P. Putnam, N.Y., 1859.
" Life of George Washington, 5 Vols., G. P. Putnam & Co., N.Y., 1856.
Prescott's Conquest of Mexico, 3 Vols., J. B. Lippincott & Co., Phila., 1861.
" Ferdinand and Isabella, 3 Vols., " " " " 1861.
" Philip II., 3 Vols., " " " " 1861.
" Conquest of Peru, 2 Vols., " " " " 1861.
" Robertson's Hist. of Charles V., 3 Vols., ' " " 1865.
Hume's History of England, 6 Vols., Harper Brothers, N.Y. 1850.
Macaulay's " " " 5 Vols,, Phillips, Sampson, & Co., Boston, 1857.
Pictorial " " " 7 Vols., la. oct., W. & R. Chambers, L'don, 1855.
Smucker's History of the Four Georges, D. Appleton & Co., N.Y., 1860.
Lancelott's Queens of England, 2 Vols., " " " 1859.
Russell's History of Modern Europe, 3 Vols., Harper Brothers, N.Y., 1857.
White's History of France, D. Appleton & Co., N.Y., 1859.
Kohlrausch's History of Germany, " " " 1855
Motley's Dutch Republic, Harper Brothers, N.Y., 1861.
" History of the United Netherlands, " " " 1860.
D'Aubigne's Hist. of the Reformation, 4 Vols. in one, Robt. Carter, N.Y., 1847.
Lamartine's History of Turkey, 3 Vols., D. Appleton & Co., N.Y., 1857.
Abbott's Empire of Austria, Mason Brothers, N.Y., 1859.
" " " Russia, " " " 1860.
Thiers' French Revolution, 4 Vols., D. Appleton & Co., N.Y., 1854.
Benton's Thirty Years in U.S. Senate, 2 Vols. " " " 1854.
Greeley's American Conflict, 2 Vols., O. D. Case & Co., Hartford, 1864, '66.
New American Cyclopædia and the Annual Cyclopædias published by D. Appleton & Co., N.Y.
Allison's Europe, Gould's abridgement, A. S. Barnes & Co., N.Y., 1853.
Mallory's Life and Speeches of Clay, 2 Vols. " " " 1857.
Weber's Outline of Universal History, Brewer & Tileston, 1860.

MODEL LESSON.

A single model lesson cannot well give all the methods to be used in class exercises; but it may serve to suggest some of the better ones. A map of England is on the black-board: the Map of Time remains rolled till after the review. The pupils are supposed to be twelve years of age. The time of the lesson is forty minutes. The class is supposed to have completed the Sixteenth Century.

Teacher. "What is the lesson for to-day?"

Class. "The first three dates in the reign of James I. of England."

Teacher. "Well; but let us first review as usual the lesson of yesterday. John; please write the events learned yesterday, in the proper places in the blank chart on the black-board. George; you may write the same events in a list with the dates in figures."

John and James write and the class watch and criticise. Often the whole class write. The Map is then unrolled, and ten minutes are spent in a spirited but careful review of the lesson of the previous day, the place of every event named being pointed out on the Map. Five minutes more are given to rapid drill on the events of the Sixteenth Century, as follows; the teacher, or one of the pupils, pointing to the years; the class follow the pointer and call out. "Francis I., 1515"; "Henry VIII., 1509"; "Charles IX., 1560"; "Charles V., 1519"; "Henry IV., 1589"; "Diet of Worms, 1521"; &c., &c. Then the teacher calling out events in rapid succession, the class, either in concert or in succession, as the teacher may direct, give the dates. Sometimes the order is changed, and the teacher calls out the dates and the class give the events. Frequently this drill should be conducted without the Map.

Teacher. "James may give the first event described in the lesson for to-day."

James recites from the Hand-Book the account of the accession of James I.

Teacher. "When did the event occur?"

Class. "In the year 1603."

The attention is carefully called to its place on the Chart and this place described as "in the first decade, third year-space, upper line, in the Seventeenth Century." The class notice that it is just one hundred years later than the marriage of James IV. of Scotland with Margaret, James' great grandmother, through whom he derived his title to the throne of England. They notice also that it is fifty years later than the accession of Mary, and forty-five years later than that of Elizabeth.

Teacher. "Has any one learned any additional facts concerning this accession of James, or concerning James himself?"

Several hands are raised, and each one, as called upon, gives his facts and the authority as follows:

1st Pupil. "Hume says James was the great grandson of Margaret, elder daughter of Henry VII., and that he was the son of Henry Stuart, Lord Darnley, also a descendent of Margaret."

2d Pupil. "The New American Cyclopædia says he was born in Edinburg Castie, June 19th, 1566, nearly one year before his mother was compelled to abdicate in his favor, making him James VI. of Scotland, and about two years before she fled to England."

3d Pupil. "His mother was a Catholic, but he was brought up as a Protestant.

4th Pupil. "Elizabeth died, March 24th. April 5th, James left Edinburg on his royal journey to London. His clumsy person and awkward manners made a very unfavorable impression on the English."

5th Pupil. "The Pictorial History of England tells amusing stories of his vanity and pedantry, and says that he was so poor that he could not begin his journey till he had received money from England."

6th Pupil. "Elizabeth left England at war with Spain, but enjoying great prosperity. James pursued a peaceful policy and closed the Spanish war."

7th Pupil. "James' chief fault, according to Macaulay, was his extravagant estimation of his royal prerogative. This made him tyrannical; but his very weakness and meanness saved England."

The contemporary events are then called for, and given as far as the class has studied them.

In a similar way each of the three dates is recited, and additional facts brought out, and the class questioned upon the whole to fasten it in memory, particular care being taken to fix the places and dates firmly in the mind. The next three dates are assigned as the lesson for the next day, and the few minutes that remain are given to the back review of the reign of Henry VIII. Each pupil is called upon to state what had been learned under some one date, and the class criticise, adding anything which is omitted. The lesson closes, when the time permits, with a drill in Historical Geography. Each pupil may have his atlas open before him, or a large map may be hung on the wall, or made on the black-board. The teacher may mention in succession places of historic interest, and the pupils give the events which occurred at these places with the dates, and also some description of the places themselves. Countries may be named and the history of their changes in territory and in government may be given. As a third exercise, the teacher names events, and the pupils describe the geographical position and relations of the events.

HAND-BOOK OF HISTORY.

GENERAL VIEW

OF THE

SIXTEENTH CENTURY.

THE SIXTEENTH CENTURY was a century of storms. Civil, religious, and intellectual struggles of immense power, and often of tornado violence, shook the whole civilized world. It was the stormy morning of modern history and civilization.

At the opening of the century, four great monarchies,—England, France, Spain, and the German Empire,—just recovered from feudal strifes and weakness, and lifted into solid form and power under the rule of monarchs of absolute temper and extraordinary ability, stood confronting each other. Near the beginning of the century, these monarchies fell into the hands of three young kings, mere boys in years, but of the most restless ambition and great energy. These were Henry VIII. of England, Francis I. of France, and Charles I. of Spain, who soon became Charles V. of Germany, uniting on the head of a boy of nineteen years, two of the mightiest crowns of Europe.

The temporal power of the Papacy, raised to unusual strength under the warlike Popes, Alexander VI. and Julius II., fell, at the same time, into the hands of the brilliant Leo X., one of the youngest of the Popes. The Turkish power just broken over the Dardanelles, with those wild waves which, again and again, rolled to the very heart of Europe, now passed from the hands of the terrible murderer, Selim I., to the young Sultan, Solyman, the Magnificent. Such monarchies and such men betokened storms;

and the wars of the League of Cambray and the Holy League, the four wars of the House of Hapsburg with France, and the Turkish wars which filled and convulsed the first half of the century, were but the natural products of the circumstances of the age.

The revival of learning, that wonderful awaking of the human mind after the sleep of the Dark Ages, received, at the close of the fifteenth century, a fresh impulse from the great discoveries of America, and of the Sea-route to the Indies, and passed over into the sixteenth, with a power that stirred the intellect of Europe in every department of life and thought. Art arose, under those great monarchs of the chisel and the brush, Michael Angelo and Raphael; Science, led by Copernicus, Galileo, and Kepler, opened new continents of learning to mankind; and Literature, nourished by the studies of such scholars as Erasmus, Luther, and Melanchthon, advanced to new realms, and opened a new era with the names of Shakespeare, Spenser, and Bacon.

But the grandest movement of the century, and that which will make it memorable among all the ages, was the Protestant Reformation. Rising like a whirlwind amid surrounding tempests, it soon absorbed within its own more tremendous and ever-widening sweep all the powers, political, intellectual, and moral, of the age; and during the latter half of the century, Europe was struggling in the tremendous grapple, already begun, between old Catholicism and young Protestantism. The chief of these religious wars were the war for civil and religious liberty in the Netherlands, under the lead of that greatest of sixteenth century statesmen, William the Silent; and the wars of the Catholic Leaguers in France, against the Huguenots, under the brave Henry of Navarre.

Save that in which the life of Jesus occurred, the world has never seen a grander century than the sixteenth.

AMERICA.

America was discovered, at the close of the fifteenth Century, (October 12th, 1492,) by Christopher Columbus. This discovery at once awakened throughout Europe the spirit of adventure and exploration. Henry VII. of England granted, in 1496, a patent of discovery to John Cabot and his three sons; and in June, 1497, Sebastian Cabot, one of these sons, discovered the American Continent at some point on the coast of Labrador. This was the first discovery of the Continent, Columbus not reaching the main-land till fourteen months later, (August, 1498,) during his third voyage. Amerigo Vespucci did not visit the Continent to which his name was unjustly given, till 1499. In January, 1500, Pinzon, one of three brothers who accompanied Columbus in his first voyage, discovered Brazil and the mouth of the Amazon. In the same year, Admiral Cabral, with a Portuguese fleet, on his way to the Cape of Good Hope, was driven by a storm on the coast of Brazil. This shows how an accident might have led to the discovery of the New World, if it had not been sooner found.

Gasper Cortereal, sent forth by Emanuel, King of Portugal,
coasted along the Continent for several hundred miles
1501. to about 50 deg. of North latitude, and, capturing fifty-
seven natives, sold them as slaves in Lisbon. On a second voyage he was lost, and the Portuguese made no further attempts at discovery in America.—*Bancroft, Vol.* 1, *p.* 14.

Columbus made his fourth and last voyage to the world he
had discovered, and which, till his death in 1506, he
1502. continued to regard as the eastern coast of Asia.—*Irving's Columbus.*

Vasco Nunez de Balboa planted on the isthmus of Darien
the first colony established on the American Conti-
1510. nent. In 1513 Balboa crossed the isthmus and discovered the Pacific Ocean.

Ponce de Leon, another Spaniard, sailing with an expedition in search of the fountain of perpetual youth, dis-
1512. covered Florida.

Hernandez de Cordova discovered the peninsula of Yucatan, now a province of Mexico, and had several encounters
1517. with the natives.—*Prescott's Conquest of Mexico, Vol.* 1.

Juan de Grijalva, having been sent out by Velasquez, the Spanish Governor of Cuba, to follow up the discoveries
1518. of Cordova, discovered Mexico.—*Prescott's Conquest of Mexico, Vol.* 1.

Magellan set forth, with five ships and two hundred and thirty-four men, to discover a western passage to the
1519. East Indies. Wintering in Patagonia, he discovered and passed through the Straits of Magellan and entered the Pacific Ocean, in October, 1520. Magellan was killed in a contest with the natives of one of the Philippine Islands, and his expedition, reduced to one ship and twenty men, in September, 1522, reached Spain, thus effecting the first circumnavigation of the world.—*Magalhaens, in Am. Cyclopedia.*

Mexico was finally conquered by the Spaniards under Hernando Cortez, after two years of bloody contest with the
1521. forces of Montezuma, its Emperor.—*Prescott's Conquest of Mexico.*

John Verrazzani, commanding an expedition fitted out by Francis I., coasted from Cape Fear River to Newfound-
1524. land, and gave the name of New France to the entire region.—*Bancroft, Vol.* 1, *p.* 15.

Pamphilo Narvaez, hoping to find another rich empire like Mexico, invaded Florida with three hundred men and
1528. forty horses, and penetrated as far as Georgia.

Francisco Pizarro, emulous of the fame and success of Cortez in Mexico, after several previous attempts, invaded
1531. and conquered Peru, the celebrated empire of the rich and civilized Incas.—*Prescott's Conquest of Peru.*

James Cartier, in a second voyage, discovered the gulf and river of St. Lawrence. He ascended the river as far as
1535. Montreal, and passed the winter at Quebec. Six years

later, 1541, Cartier, under Lord Roberval, attempted, but in vain, to plant a settlement at Quebec.—*Bancroft, Vol.* 1, *pp.* 19–24.

Cortez visited and explored the Gulf of California. Lower
1536. California is said to have been discovered two years earlier by one Zimenes.

Ferdinand De Soto, another would-be conqueror, landed in
1541. Florida June 10, 1539, with six hundred men, and passed four years exploring the country embraced in the present States of Georgia, Alabama, and Mississippi, and fighting with the Indians. In 1541 he discovered the Mississippi. After wintering with his army in Arkansas, they returned to the Mississippi, where De Soto died, and was buried in the great river he had discovered.—*Bancroft, Vol.* 1, *pp.* 41–59.

This closed for many years the attempts of the Spaniards to explore or make conquests in North America. Their monarch, Charles V., was too fully occupied with his wars, and with the reformation in his German empire, to attend much to the far-off, new world.—*Robertson's Charles V.*

The Huguenots, exposed to great persecutions in France,
1562. attempted a settlement at Port Royal. The first settlers soon left, and a second settlement was made by another party on St. John's river in 1564.—*Bancroft, Vol.* 1, *pp.* 61–71.

The Spaniards, under Pedro Melendes, founded the city of St.
1565. Augustine, and attacked and destroyed the Huguenot settlement. St. Augustine was the first permanent settlement in the United States.—*Bancroft, Vol.* 1.

Martin Frobisher, an English navigator, penetrated Frobish-
1576. er's Strait in search of a northwest passage. This was the first of that long series of attempts, ending with Sir John Franklin's fatal expedition, to discover a northern route to the Pacific Ocean.—*Bancroft, Vol.* 1, *page* 81.

Frobisher, with fifteen ships, visited the region of Hudson's
1578. Straits to found a settlement and gather gold. The expedition, after many misfortunes, returned to England, and the project was abandoned.

This same year, Sir Humphrey Gilbert obtained a patent, under which he made an unsuccessful attempt to effect a settlement within the region of the United States.—*Bancroft, Vol.* 1.

Sir Francis Drake, an English freebooter, visited the coasts
of California and Oregon, and circumnavigated the
1579. world. His voyage commenced in 1577, and terminated in 1580.—*Bancroft, Vol.* 1, *page* 86.

Sir Walter Raleigh, having obtained from Elizabeth a patent,
dated March 25, sent out two ships under Captains
1584. Amidas and Barlow. The expedition explored Albemarle and Pamlico Sounds, and Roanoke Island, and then returned with glowing accounts of the country to England.

Raleigh, at much expense, fitted out seven ships and one
hundred and eight colonists to make a settlement. Af-
1585. ter spending a year in the country, the settlers were carried back to England by Sir F. Drake. The undiscouraged Raleigh continued for several years to send out ships and men to renew the attempt at settlements, till, impoverished by immense expenditures, he was forced to abandon the attempt; and thus the century closed without witnessing a single permanent English colony in America, or a single permanent settlement within the original limits of the United States.—*Bancroft, Vol.* 1, *pp.* 95–108.

N. B. The references to authorities, under the several dates, are confined to a few books of easy accessibility. Many of the events can be found in the common school abridgements now in use, such as Lossing's, Willson's, Willard's, Anderson's, and Goodrich's School Histories.

ENGLAND.

THE SIXTEENTH CENTURY, in England, was the century of the Tudors, an astute, active, enterprising, but cautious and grasping family. The opening of the century found Henry the Seventh, the first of the House of Tudor, on the throne. England, under his firm but despotic rule, rapidly recovered from the terrible desolations of the War of the Roses, which he finished at the battle of Bosworth Field in 1485, and speedily mounted to the rank of a first-class Power. It seems to have been the settled policy of the Tudors to attend, first of all, to their own affairs, and thus England during their reigns took but little part in the great struggles which shook the continent during this century. When it did interfere it was with a careful eye to its own aggrandizement.

Like other founders of dynasties, Henry was anxious to secure family alliances with other reigning houses, and in 1501 he effected a marriage of his eldest son, Arthur, with Catherine of Aragon. Arthur died the next year, and the King compelled his remaining son, young Henry, twelve years of age, to espouse the widow, then eighteen.—*Hume's England, Vol.* 3.

Henry's eldest daughter, Margaret, married James IV. of Scotland. Just a century later, a great grandson of
1503. Margaret, the first Stuart, ascended the English throne and united England and Scotland under one King.—*Hume, Vol.* 3.

Henry VII. died April 21, and his son, "Bluff Hal," a rash and ruddy boy of nearly eighteen years, was crowned as
1509. Henry VIII. He immediately celebrated his nuptials with Catherine, his brother's widow, and the two were crowned together.—*Hume, Vol.* 3. *Lancelott's Queens of England, Vol.* 1.

Henry was persuaded to join the Holy League and declare war against France. His father-in-law, the crafty Fer-
1511. dinand of Spain, induced him to send an English army into the south of France, in 1512, and then took advantage of its presence to secure for himself the Kingdom of Navarre.—*Ferdinand and Isabella, Vol.* 3, *pp.* 350–356.

The battle of Flodden Field was fought September 9, between the Scots under James IV. and the English under the
1513. Earl of Surrey. Henry was still in France. James himself, with many of the principal nobility of Scotland, fell. The Scots lost 10,000, the English about 7,000 men.—*Hume's History. Flodden Field in American Cyclopedia.*

Thomas Wolsey, the arrogant but able prelate and statesman of Henry's reign, was made a Cardinal by the Pope,
1515. and created by Henry, Lord Chancellor of England.

He was for nearly fourteen years the real ruler of the Kingdom. —*Wolsey, in American Cyclopedia.*

Wolsey, failing finally to favor the divorce which Henry was bent on obtaining from Catherine of Aragon, fell into
1530. disfavor, was in 1529 deprived of his dignities, and in November, 1530, died on his way to London to answer to the charge of high treason.—*Hume, Vol.* 3.

Henry was divorced from the good, but injured Catherine, and married Anne Boleyn, who, a few months later, gave
1533. birth to Elizabeth, afterwards Queen of England.—*Queens of England, Vol.* 1.

Henry's quarrel with Rome having became irreconcilable, he declared himself the head of the Church in England,
1534. and procured acts of Parliament making it a crime to acknowledge the authority of the Pope. This placed England on the Protestant side of the great religious struggles of the age, though Henry by no means adopted the Protestant doctrines.—*Hume's England, Vol.* 3.

Queen Anne, having been convicted, falsely, it is now believed, of corrupt conduct, was beheaded May 19, and three
1536. days afterward, Henry married Jane Seymour.—*Queens of England, Vol.* 1.

October 12 Prince Edward was born, and a few days afterwards his mother, Queen Jane, died. She was the most
1537. beloved by Henry of all his wives.

Henry married Anne of Cleves, whom he divorced the same year, and took as his fifth wife Catherine Howard, July
1540. —, 1540. This marriage was followed by a furious persecution of both Protestants and Catholics. Queen Catherine was beheaded February 12, 1542.—*Queens of England, Vol.* 1. *Hume, Vol.* 3.

James V. of Scotland, a Catholic, sent an army of 10,000 men to revenge the insult of a foray made by the English on
1542. the Scottish border. They were met by about five hundred English soldiers at Solway Moss, November 25, and being thrown into a panic, ran away with a loss of a few killed, and many prisoners. James, greatly mortified, died a few days af-

terwards, December 14, leaving his crown to his infant daughter, the celebrated and unfortunate Mary, Queen of Scots. Henry immediately proposed the marriage of his son Edward with the infant Queen, but a French alliance was preferred, and Henry, in consequence, joined the German Emperor, Charles V., against Francis I. A war with France ensued, but without any important results.—*Strickland's Queens of Scotland. Hume, Vol.* 3.

Henry married his sixth and last wife, Catherine Parr, a Protestant. She survived him, though at one time she was
1543. threatened with impeachment.—*Queens of Eng., Vol.* 1.

Henry VIII. died January 28, and his son Edward, then only a little over nine years old, was proclaimed King of
1547. England. The Duke of Somerset was appointed protector. The Protestant party gained great power during Edward's reign, and the Episcopal church was more fully organized by Archbishop Cranmer. Another war with Scotland occurred the first year of this reign.

On the death of Edward VI., July 6, his eldest sister, Mary, daughter of Catherine of Aragon, was proclaimed Queen.
1553. Mary was a Catholic, and her accession caused great alarm among the Protestants, giving rise to serious revolts. Lady Jane Grey, a great grand-daughter of Henry VII., was proclaimed Queen by the arts of her father-in-law, the Duke of Northumberland, and in consequence was beheaded, Feb. 12, 1554.—*Hume's England, Vol.* 3.

Mary married Philip II. of Spain, who had been made King of Naples by his father, Charles V., to raise him to an
1554. equal dignity with his royal wife. Under Philip's influence, severe persecutions of the Protestants ensued. Archbishop Cranmer, and bishops Latimer and Ridley, with many others, were burnt at the stake. Philip left England in September, 1555, and never revisited his wife except once, in 1557, to engage England to take part in his war against France.—*Hume's England, Vol.* 3. *Prescott's Philip II., Vol.* 1, *Chaps.* 4 *and* 7.

Elizabeth, called by her subjects the "good Queen Bess," succeeded to the Crown on the death of her sister Ma-
1558. ry, November 17. Her reign was one of the longest

and most brilliant in England's history. The names of such men as Shakespeare, Bacon, Spenser, and Ben Jonson made the Elizabethan age one of the most famous also in literature. Her accession threw England again on the side of the Protestants in the great religious conflicts of the age. She lent a cautious, but still effective, support to the Protestant parties in the Netherlands, France, and Scotland.

1559. John Knox, the leader of the reformation in Scotland, after some years of exile, spent, in part, with Calvin at Geneva, returned to Perth. A fierce struggle immediately broke out between the Protestants and the Catholic Queen regent. The Protestants received aid from Elizabeth, and the Catholics from France. The Protestant party triumphed, and Scotland took its place on the side of the Protestant Powers. *John Knox in American Cyclopedia. Hume's England, Vol.* 4.

1561. Francis Bacon, afterwards Lord Chancellor of England, the great founder of modern Philosophy and Science, was born January 22, and died April 9, 1626. His works changed the current of human thought, and gave rise to modern learning.—*Bacon in American Cyclopedia.*

1564. William Shakespeare, the great dramatist, was born at Stratford-on-Avon, April 23, and died April 23, 1616. His fame as a writer is unsurpassed by that of any uninspired writer the world has ever seen.—*Shakespeare in American Cyclopedia.*

1568. Mary, Queen of Scots, after the death of her husband, Francis II., returned to Scotland, and married first in 1565, Lord Darnley, and after his murder, in 1567, she married his reputed murderer, Bothwell. Her marriages and her attempts to restore the Catholic faith occasioned revolts, and her forces being beaten in battle, she fled to England, where she was held captive by Elizabeth for nineteen years.—*Hume's England, Vol.* 4.

1587. Mary, being finally convicted of conspiring against the life of Elizabeth, was beheaded February 8, in the forty-fifth year of her age. Historians disagree as to her guilt. She doubtless fell a victim to what was thought at the time a necessary state policy. The real contest was between the two religions. Had Mary, who was next heir to the crown, succeeded Elizabeth, violent efforts would have been made to restore the Catholics to power, and suppress Protestantism.—*Hume's England, Vol.* 4. *Mary Stuart in American Cyclopedia.*

The Spanish Armada, the greatest fleet which had ever ap-
1588. peared on the ocean up to that time, was sent by Philip II. to conquer England, and restore it to the Catholic faith. It consisted of 130 vessels, carrying 2,638 guns, and nearly 30,000 men. It was shattered by tempests, and defeated by the English.

Elizabeth's zeal for Protestantism was stimulated to greater
1591. activity by this attempt of Philip, and she readily lent her aid to Henry IV. and the French Huguenots, who were engaged in a deadly struggle with the Catholic league in France.—*Hume, Vol.* 4, *page* 274.

The first East India Company was formed, for trading with
1600. the countries east of the Cape of Good Hope. Great commercial corporations for trading with, settling, and governing, distant lands, constituted a prominent feature of the times. The French, Spaniards, Portuguese, and Dutch had these companies. This English company and its successors gave to England the mighty empire it now holds in Southern Asia.—*East India Companies in American Cyclopedia.*

FRANCE.

THE OPENING of the sixteenth century found France great and powerful. Her turbulent nobility had been subdued by the iron hand of Louis the eleventh. The throne was filled by an able and just monarch, Louis XII., called the "Father of his People." His marriage with Anne of Brittany, the widow of his predecessor, Charles VIII., had consolidated the Kingdom; he had again recovered Milan and Florence, in Italy, and he stood ready to resist the attacks that threatened him from jealous rivals.

The French monarch, claiming the Kingdom of Naples and Sicily, united with Ferdinand of Spain to conquer and
1501. partition this Kingdom. The conquest being made, the crafty Ferdinand snatched the prize, and became King of Naples and the Sicilies.—*Prescott's Ferd. and Isab., Vol.* 3, *Chap.* 10.

This was followed by a war, in which Gonsalvo, the "Great Captain," won honor and victory for the Spanish arms.—*Ibid, Chaps.* 11 *and* 13.

Louis gave his neice, Germane de Foix, a girl of eighteen, to Ferdinand as a wife, and remitted his claim on the crown
1505. of Naples as her dower. This closed, for a time, the French attempts to regain the control of that Kingdom. *Ibid, Chap.* 17. *White's France.*

Louis, to indemnify himself for the loss of Naples, formed, December 10, with Maximilian, of Germany, the League
1508. of Cambray, in which the Pope, and Ferdinand, and other princes, were induced to take part, to recover from the rich and proud republic of Venice the territories of which she had despoiled the church, and other parties.—*Ferdinand and Isabella, Vol.* 3, *Chap.* 22.

Early in April, Louis crossed the Alps with an army which conquered all opposition. "City and castle fell before
1509. him." On the 14th of May, he fought the battle of Agnadello, which broke the power of Venice, and compelled her to relinquish all her continental possessions.—*Ferdinand and Isabella, Vol.* 3, *Chap.* 22. *Russell's Modern Europe, Vol.* 1, *Letter* 54.

Louis' successes roused Pope Julius, who, making peace with Venice, formed the Holy League to expel the French
1511. from Italy. To meet the forces of this league, Louis despatched the young Duke of Nemours, Gaston de Foix, the Napoleon of his age.

The battle of Ravenna, one of the bloodiest conflicts on record, was fought April 12. The French gained a com-
1512. plete victory, but lost all their advantages by the death

of their great leader, the young de Foix, who was slain in the battle. They retreated to the foot of the Alps, and abandoned all their conquests in the north of Italy.—*Ferd. and Isabella, Vol.* 3, *Chap.* 22. *White's France, p.* 219.

Louis XII. died January 1, 1515, and was succeeded by his
cousin and son-in-law, Francis I., a handsome, brave,
1515. and willful youth of 20 years.

Francis I., immediately on his accession, planned the recovery of Milan; and having passed the Alps, he met the Swiss troops at Marignano, September 13, and defeated them in a battle so fiercely fought as to have gained in history the title of the "Battle of the Giants." This restored Milan to France.—*Russell's Modern Europe, Vol.* 1, *Letter* 55.

The magnificent meeting of Francis I. and Henry VIII. at
the "Field of the Cloth of Gold," near Ardres, was
1520. planned by Francis to win Henry to his side in his anticipated struggle with Charles V. of Germany. The meeting impoverished many of the nobles of both Kingdoms, but failed to secure its object.—*Hume's Eng., Vol.* 3. *White's France, p.* 230.

The first of the wars between Francis and his great rival, the
Emperor Charles V., was begun by an attempt of Fran-
1521. cis to recover Navarre from the Spaniards. These wars occupied the attention of the Emperor, and gave the Reformation time to gain a foothold in the Empire.—*Robertson's Charles V, Book* 2. *Kohlrausch's Germany,* (*Appleton,*) *p.* 263.

Charles V., by a personal visit to England, induced Henry
VIII. to take part in the war against Francis. The
1522. English invaded Picardy, but retired with heavy losses. —*Hume's England, Vol.* 3. *Robertson's Charles V, Book* 2.

Charles, intoxicated with the successes he had gained over
the French in Italy, sent an army to invade Provence
1524. and besiege Marseilles. The siege lasted forty days, when the imperial forces were compelled to retire.—*Charles V, Book* 4. *Kohlrausch's Germany, p.* 264.

Francis, taking courage, again invaded Italy, and recovering
Milan, laid siege to Pavia. The imperialists finally at-
1525. tempting to relieve the garrison, the battle of Pavia

was fought February 24. Francis' army was totally routed, and himself taken prisoner. It was a fatal day for France.—*Charles V, Book* 4. *White's France, Chap.* 9.

The peace of Madrid, concluded by the captive Francis, and his triumphant rival, Charles, closed the first of their
1526. wars, and restored the French King to liberty.—*Charles V, Book* 4. *White's France.*

Francis, disregarding the treaty which had been forced from him, formed a league with the Pope, Venice, and Milan,
1527. against the Emperor, which led to the opening of the second war. The Duke of Bourbon, a renegade Frenchman, commanding the Emperor's forces, May 6, attacked Rome and took it by a furious assault, in which Bourbon fell. The city was sacked with gross outrage and cruelty.—*Charles V, Book* 1.

A peace was finally made at Cambray through the agency of Charles' aunt, and Francis' mother. The peace was
1529. hence called the "Ladies' Peace." In this peace Francis relinquished all his Italian claims.—*Charles V, Book* 5. *White's France, Chap* 2. *Kohlrausch's Germany, p.* 266.

During the absence of Charles V., who was conducting an expedition against Tunis and Algiers, Francis I. revived
1536. his claims in Italy, and raising an army, invaded Savoy. Charles returning, took up arms in behalf of the Duke of Savoy, and invaded Southern France with fifty thousand men. Thus opened the third great war between these rivals. Francis repelled the invasion as the Russians of a later time repelled the French, by desolating his country before the invaders. The French monarch also shocked all Europe by forming a league with Solyman II., the Turk, against Charles.—*Russell's Modern Europe, Vol.* 1, *Letter* 59. *Charles V, Book* 5.

Both parties becoming tired and exhausted by the war, consented, June 18, to a truce for ten years. The truce of
1538. Nice was effected by the agency of the Pope, Paul III., who acted as umpire.—*Charles V. White's France.*

The Emperor, having been weakened by a second, and, this time, unfortunate expedition against Algiers, Francis
1542. took occasion, from the murder of two of his ambassa-

dors by Charles' soldiers, to declare war a fourth time. He sent five armies into the field. The hostilities that followed were of no permanent consequence, and were not distinguished by any event of much note except the great victory of Cerisoles, which the French gained over the imperial forces April 11, 1544. *Russell's Europe, Vol.* 1, *Letter* 59. *Charles V, Book* 7.

The peace of Crespy, concluded between Francis and Charles,
September 18, closed the war. The Protestant power
1544. had been growing, almost unchecked, during these bloody
struggles, and both the Emperor and the French King were becoming alarmed. Henceforward they became allies rather than rivals in their zeal against the new heresy.—*White's France, p.* 244. *Charles V, Book* 7.

On the 31st of March, in this year, Francis I. died, and was
succeeded on the throne by his son, Henry II., the hus-
1547. band of the celebrated Catherine de Medici, one of the
most able and infamous women in history.—*Catherine de Medici in American Cyclopedia. White's France.*

Henry II., while bitterly persecuting the Protestants of France,
having formed a league with Maurice of Saxony, declar-
1552. ed war against the Emperor, who was wholly unprepared.
The French entered Lorraine almost without opposition, and took Metz, Toul, and Verdun, while Maurice pressing, and nearly capturing Charles, compelled him to the treaty of Passau, which secured religious liberty to the German Protestants. The war between Henry and the Emperor went on till the truce of Vancelles, 1556, the French defending their conquests and making new ones in Italy.—*Russell's Mod. Europe, Vol.* 1, *Letter* 61. *Prescott's Philip II., Vol.* 1, *Chap.* 5. *Charles V, Book* 10.

Henry II., instigated by the Pope, soon broke his truce, and
recommenced the war; but now with Philip II. and
1557. Spain as his foes, and with the Pope and the Turks as
his allies. England aided Spain. The united Spanish and English armies invaded France and besieged St. Quentin, before whose walls a great battle was fought August 10, in which the French suffered a disastrous defeat. This defeat was followed by others, and in 1559 the peace of Chateau Cambressis

closed the war.—*Philip II., Vol.* 1, *pp.* 225–284. *Modern Europe, Vol.* 1, *Letter* 63.

Henry II. died of a wound received at a tournament, and his
1559. son, Francis II., a sickly boy of sixteen, succeeded to the throne.—*White's France.*

Francis died, poisoned, it is believed, with the connivance of
1560. his mother. His brother, Charles IX., ten years old, became King, his mother being regent.

The terrible religious wars in France between the Huguenot
1562. or Protestant party, and the Catholics, broke out with the massacre of the Protestants at Vassy. Fourteen armies were levied and put in motion at once, and France was desolated for years by these struggles.—*Modern Europe, Vol.* 1, *Letter* 66. *White's France, Chap.* 2.

On the 20th of August, St. Bartholomew's day, a great slaugh-
1572. ter of the Protestants was made in Paris and other cities of France, by order of the King, under the influence of his fiendish mother, Catherine de Medici.—*White's France, Chap.* 11.

Charles IX., conscience stricken for his great crime, died two
1574. years after the massacre, not without suspicion of having been poisoned by his mother. His brother, Henry III., who had been King of Poland, succeeded him on the throne, a poor, weak, wicked monarch, under the control of his infamous mother.—*White's France.*

A league of the Catholics, under Henry, Duke of Guise, was
1576. formed to exterminate the Protestants, and to prevent the accession of the Protestant Henry of Navarre, the next heir to the crown. War followed with increasing violence and hatred.

The King, hating the ambitious and arrogant Guise, threw
1585. himself into the hands of Henry of Navarre, and the war of the Three Henrys broke out.

The mob of Paris rose in favor of Guise, barricaded the
1588. streets, and massacred the royal guards. The King fled from Paris. Henry of Guise was slain shortly afterwards by the King's command.

Henry III. was assassinated, and the brilliant and popular Henry of Navarre assumed the title of Henry IV. He
1589. was the first of the Bourbons. The war only became more violent on his accession.—*Henry IV. in Am. Cyc. White's France.*

At the battle of Ivry, fought March 13, Henry defeated the army of the League. After this battle he besieged Paris,
1590. then in the hands of the leaguers. The siege was raised by the Duke of Parma, who had been sent by Philip II. with a Spanish army to invade France.—*White's France.*

Elizabeth, who had repeatedly aided the Huguenots, sent new succors to Henry, who, with their aid, laid siege to Rouen,
1591. but was driven from his anticipated prize by the Duke of Parma.—*Hume's England, Vol.* 4.

Henry, finding he could not overcome the opposition by fighting, finally professed to be converted to Catholicism,
1593. and the next year, the Catholic towns submitted, and he was crowned King of France, February 27th. He was one of the most able and popular Kings that ever ruled in France.—*White's France, Chap.* 12.

Henry was aided both in conquering and in governing his Kingdom by Maximilian de Bethune, Baron de Rosny,
1597. Duke of Sully, one of the purest and greatest statesman of his age. He was made minister of finance, and speedily raised France to a high position of prosperity. Henry made him Duke of Sully in 1606.—*Sully in Am. Cyc. White's France.*

The 13th of April, Henry issued the celebrated Edict of Nantes, granting religious freedom and toleration to the
1598. Protestants. On the 2d of May he concluded the peace of Vervins with Philip II. Thus closed this long stormy period, and France had peace again.—*White's France.*

SPAIN AND PORTUGAL.

In the last decade of the fifteenth century, two events of vast importance helped to lift Spain into great power. The old Spanish Kingdom of Aragon, and those of Castile and Leon, having been united by the marriage of their respective sovereigns, Ferdinand and Isabella, succeeded, in 1492, in conquering the Moors, who for eight hundred years had held the fairest provinces of Spain. In the same memorable year, Columbus discovered America, and added a new world to the Spanish dominions. Portugal had taken a prominent part in the great maritime discoveries of the fifteenth century. At the opening of the sixteenth, she had just passed the Cape of Good Hope, and was beginning the famous Portuguese empire in the Indies.

The Kingdom of Naples and Sicily had long been under the rule of a dynasty of Aragonese kings. Ferdinand uni-
1501. ted with France to seize and partition it between them. Out of this grew the war in which the celebrated Gonsalvo de Cordova, "the Great Captain," gained such renown, and which resulted in adding the crown of Naples and Sicily to Spain.—*Prescott's Ferd. and Isabella, Vol.* 3.

The good Isabella died, and the crown of Castile and Leon descended to her daughter, Joanna. Ferdinand at first
1504. became regent, but afterwards Joanna's husband, Philip I., son of Maximilian I. of Germany, was recognized.—*Ferd. and Isabella, Vol.* 3.

Ferdinand married the young and beautiful Germane de Foix, and her uncle, Louis XII., relinquished to her as a mar-
1505. riage dower the French claims upon Naples.—*See France.*

Ximenes de Cisneros, a great statesman, and an austere prelate, was made a Cardinal, and appointed Inquisitor
1507. General. He had been confessor to Isabella, and was virtually regent of Castile after her death. His name is famous in Spanish history.—*Ferd. and Isa., Vols.* 2 *and* 3. *Charles V., Book* 1. *For his death and character, see Vol.* 3, *Chap.* 25.

The Portuguese having made the conquest of India, Albuquerque, the bold and enterprizing viceroy, seized upon
1510. the rich and flourishing city of Goa, and made it the capital of the Portuguese possessions.—*Albuquerque in Am. Cyc. Mod. Europe, Vol.* 1, *Letter* 57.

Albuquerque visited Malacca with a marauding party of eight Portuguese and two hundred Natives, and, capturing the
1511. chief town, took from it immense booty, the king's fifth amounting to $5,000,000.—*Albuquerque in American Cy.*

On the 23d of January, Ferdinand, the Catholic and the crafty, died, and the crowns of Ferdinand and Isabella were
1516. permanently united on the head of their grandson, Charles of Austria, son of Philip I. and Joanna. Charles I. was sixteen years of age at his accession to the then mightiest throne in the world. United Spain, the Kingdom of Navarre, the Kingdom of Naples and the Sicilies, the Kingdom of the Netherlands, large territories in the northern part of Africa, and the American continent, were embraced in his empire, and he was prospective heir to rich territories of Austria and Germany. —*Robertson's Charles V., Book* 1.

Cardinal Ximenes was appointed regent by the will of Ferdinand, and he ruled with great ability and success till Charles came into Spain.—*Ferd. and Isa., Vol.* 3, *Chap.* 5.

Charles I. was elected to succeed his paternal grandfather, Maximilian I., and became Emperor Charles V., the ti-
1519. tle by which he is best known in history. During his reign, the fortunes of Spain were linked with those of the German Empire, and the events need not be enumerated here.—*Charles V., Book* 1.

Charles V. abdicated the throne of Spain and the Netherlands in favor of his son, the young and bigoted Philip II.,
1556. who had previously, in 1554, received the crown of Naples on the occasion of his marriage with Queen Mary of England. Under Philip, Spanish history began to run in its own separate channel again, and Spain to decline.—*Prescott's Philip II., Vol.* 1. *Charles V., Book* 12.

Battle of St. Quentin, 1557. See account under France.

Philip appointed his half-sister Margaret, Duchess of Parma,
1559. regent of the Netherlands, and left that country, never to return. From his palace, in Spain, he undertook to manage the Netherland affairs, and soon aroused, by his tyranny, that mighty struggle for liberty, which outlasted his reign, and ended by separating this great province from his kingdom. The events of this struggle belong rather to the history of the Netherlands.—*Philip II., Vol.* 1. *Dutch Republic, Vol.* 1.

The other leading features of Philip's reign were the rebellion of the Moriscoes or Moors, who still remained scattered in great numbers through their ancient kingdom of Granada, and were driven in 1559 to revolt by his absurd and bigoted tyranny; the wars with the Turks, who under Selim II., were engaged in European conquest; the conquest of Portugal; and the attempted invasion of England.—*Prescott's Philip II., Vol.* 3. *Hume's England, Vol.* 4.

Spain having formed a Holy League with Venice and the
1571. Pope, against the Turks, fitted out on immense fleet under Philip's half brother, Don John of Austria. The great and decisive naval battle of Lepanto was fought on the 7th of October. It was a terrible blow to the power of the Turks, who lost their fleet and 30,000 men. But they soon rallied and renewed the war, and were finally the victors.—*Philip II., Vol.* 3. *Modern Europe, Vol.* 1, *Let.* 68.

On the death of Don Henry, King of Portugal, without heirs,
1580. Philip claimed the crown, and sent Duke Alva with an army, who overran the kingdom and vanquished all opposition. Portugal remained for the next sixty years a part of Spain.—*Mod. Europe, Vol.* 1, *Let.* 69.

Philip, hating England for its Protestantism, angry with
1588. Elizabeth because of the aid she had given to his Netherland subjects, and specially enraged by the execution of Mary, Queen of Scots, collected an immense fleet, which he styled the Invincible Armada, to invade and conquer England. The attempt failed, the fleet was destroyed, and the naval power of Spain was hopelessly crippled.—*Hume's England, Vol.* 4, *pp.* 253—263.

Philip, having declared himself defender of the Catholic
League in France, sent a Spanish army under the Duke
1590. of Parma, who compelled Henry IV. to raise the siege
of Paris.—*White's France. Mod. Europe, Vol.* 1.

Henry the next year laid siege to Rouen, but again the Duke
of Parma appeared with a Spanish army and compelled
1591. him to relinquish his nearly won prize.

The rich Spanish and Portuguese possessions, in the East
Indies, were attacked by the Dutch, who made them-
1595. selves masters of the East India trade, and established
themselves in the Island of Java.—*Modern Europe, Vol.* 1, *Let.* 71.

The peace of Vervins, made May 2d, closed the war which
had raged between France and Spain since 1595. In
1598. September, Philip II. died detested by mankind. He
was succeeded by his feeble son, Philip III., and Spain went
rapidly on to ruin.—*Mod. Europe, Vol.* 1, *Let.* 71.

THE GERMAN EMPIRE.

THE OLD GERMANIC ROMAN EMPIRE was still in existence at the opening of the sixteenth century, though it possessed but a shadow of its ancient power. Its territory embraced most of the states and kingdoms now included in Austria, Prussia, Eastern France, and Northern Italy; but its separate parts were independent sovereignties, and only acknowledged, in some general affairs, the authority of the Empire. The Emperor, who held his crown for life, was elected by seven of the chief princes who hence bore the title of Electors. For a considerable period, the Emperors had been chosen from the celebrated House of Hapsburg; and the hereditary Duke of Austria, in 1493, Maximilian I., sometimes called "Max the Penniless," was elected to succeed his father, Frederick III.—*Prescott's Robertson's Charles V., Vol.* 1, *pp.* 200—216.

Maximilian formed, with Louis XII., the League of Cambray

against Venice, in hopes to recover some of the ter-
1508. ritories the Venetians had taken from the Empire.—
Kohlrausch's Germany, Chap. 15.

The Reformation Begins.

The Reformation is usually dated from the 31st of October,
when Luther affixed his ninety-five theses, or proposi-
1517. tions against the sale of indulgences, to the door of
the church in Wittenberg. This properly begins the great era of modern history.—*Kohlrausch, Chap.* 17. *Prescott's Charles V., Vol.* 1, *p.* 532. *D'Aubigne's Hist. of Reformation.*

Luther was summoned to appear before Cardinal Cajetan,
the legate of the Pope, to answer for his heresies.
1518. Repairing to Augsburg, Luther offered arguments to
defend his views; Cajetan attempted to extort a recantation. Luther resisted, and thus won the first battle in the Reformation.—*D'Aubigne, Book* 4.

The next year, 1519, Luther met Dr. John Eck, at Leipsic, and discussed with him the doctrines he had proclaimed. It was the second battle, and again Luther triumphed.—*D'Aubigne, Book* 5.

Charles I. of Spain, grandson of Maximilian I., and also of
Ferdinand and Isabella, was elected Emperor, June 28,
1519. over his great rival Francis I., of France. He was
known in history as Charles V. of Germany, and was the greatest monarch of that age.—*Prescott's Charles V., Vol.* 1, *p.* 499.

The Pope, having issued a bull excommunicating Luther as a
heretic, and ordering his writings to be publicly burned,
1520. Luther replied by burning the Pope's bull. This was
the declaration of open war, and the Reformation entered upon its second period.—*D'Aubigne, Book* 6.

Luther was now summoned to appear before the Emperor
and the Imperial Diet at Worms. The meeting is
1521. famous in history. Luther defended his doctrines.
After his departure, the Emperor pronounced the ban of the Empire against him. But several of the princes had become his disciples and friends, and Charles being soon after involved in

his first war with Francis I., Luther escaped, and the Reformation went on.—*Prescott's Charles V., Vol.* 1, *p.* 584.

For the several wars of Charles with Francis, see France in this hand-book.

Discontents which had long existed among the peasantry of Germany finally broke out into open war. The revolt
1524. was suppressed with great slaughter. It is said that 100,000 peasants perished.—*Kohlrausch, Chap.* 17.

Lewis II., King of Hungary and Bohemia, having fallen in the great battle of Mohacz, his brother-in-law, Ferdi-
1526. nand, Archduke of Austria and brother of Charles V., succeeded to the throne of Hungary and Bohemia, thus adding these kingdoms to the Austrian States. The Turks, who were pushing their conquests up the Danube, seized several towns and carried 200,000 of the Hungarians into captivity.—*Prescott's Charles Vol.* 2, *p.* 163.

In the second war between Charles and Francis, the Pope having taken the side of France, Charles called to his
1527. aid the German Protestants, and these with his Spanish troops attacked and captured Rome. Thus the storm which was prepared for the Reform burst on the Papacy. Rome was sacked with every cruelty and indignity, and the Reform gathered strength. See the brilliant account in *D'Aubigne, Book* 13.

After the close of the second war with Francis, by the peace of Cambray, the Emperor summoned a Diet at Spires.
1529. At this meeting the Lutheran Princes presented their celebrated protest against the decrees of the Diet, and hence arose, the name Protestants, which soon became the common name of all the reformers.—*Kohlrausch, Chap.* 18. *D'Aubigne, Book* 13.

The Emperor held a grand Diet at Augsburg. Both the Protestant and Catholic princes were present in full force;
1530. the Protestants demanding toleration, and the Catholics demanding that heresy should be suppressed. The Protestants presented their confession of faith, drawn up by Melanchthon, and henceforward the Reformation had a clear and declared

body of doctrine. It now entered its third stage. It was no longer the conflict of Luther against the Pope; but of one religion and creed against another.—*Kohlrausch, Chap.* 18. *D'Aubigne, Book* 14. *Charles V., Vol.* 2, *p.* 211.

The Protestant Princes soon became aware that the Emperor would attempt to suppress the reformation, and, renew-
1531. ing their confederacy, formed the League of Smalcald. —*Kohlrausch, Chap.* 18.

In the city of Munster, arose a set of fanatics, who, pushing the doctrines of the reformation to a licentious extreme,
1534. seized the political power and committed great enormities. These "madmen of Munster" were finally suppressed in 1535, by the united power of the German Princes.—*Prescott's Charles V., Vol.* 2, *pp.* 233–245.

The city of Ghent, refusing to pay a heavy tax laid upon it, rose in revolt. The Emperor marched in person to sup-
1539. press the rebellion, and tyrannically deprived the city of all its ancient privileges. The seeds of discontent thus sown, helped to rouse the Netherlands to revolt in the next reign. —*Charles V., Vol.* 2, *p.* 334.

Luther, the great leader of the Reformation, died at Eisleben, February 18. His death did not check the progress of
1546. that great movement which he had started. He had always opposed any appeal to arms to support the reformation.

Shortly after Luther's death, a war broke out between the Emperor and the Smalcald Leaguers. The forces of the League were soon scattered by dissensions, and the Emperor, assisted by Maurice of Saxony, who had deserted his Protestant friends, soon overran the whole country, and put Spanish garrisons in the chief cities.—*Kohl. Chap.* 19. *Chas. V., Vol.* 2, *pp.* 485–513.

Maurice of Saxony, taking offence at the Emperor, formed a secret treaty with Henry II. of France against the
1551. Empire.—*Kohlrausch.*

Maurice concealed his plans till he was fully ready, and then attacked the Emperor, and nearly captured him. Char-
1552. les was forced to conclude the treaty of Passau, which gave religious peace and toleration to the Protestants.

The Diet assembled at Augsburg and confirmed the religious
toleration granted in the peace of Passau. The reform-
1555. tion was triumphant.—*Kohlrausch, Chap.* 20.

Charles V., wearied by his long and warlike reign, abdicated
his throne, appointing his son Philip II., King of his
1556. Spanish dominions, and his brother Ferdinand, Emperor of Germany, subject to the will of the electors. The empire, however, continued to be governed in Charles' name till his death in 1558.—*Prescott's Charles V., Vol.* 3.

Ferdinand I. was elected Emperor in place of his brother
Charles V. He was a mild and peaceful ruler, and
1558. permitted all parties to enjoy their own belief. Protestants, no longer kept together by a common danger, fell into endless disputes, and divided into sects; and the Jesuits, who had arisen in 1540, soon checked the further spread of the reform.—*Kohlrausch, Chap.* 21.

Ferdinand I. died July 15th, and was succeeded by his son,
Maximilian II., under whose mild and paternal rule,
1564. Germany continued to enjoy a long needed peace.

On the death of Maximilian, he was succeeded by his son,
Rodolph II., who, giving his attention more to astrology
1576. and kindred sciences than to public affairs, prepared, by his neglect, the tempests which a little later desolated his country. Germany seemed now to pause while the great battles of liberty were being fought in the Netherlands.—*Kohlrausch, Chap.* 21.

NETHERLANDS AND HOLLAND.

The Netherlands, at the opening of the Sixteenth Century, were under the government of Maximilian I. of Germany, he having married Mary of Burgundy, the heiress of the Netherlands. The sovereignty of these provinces passed by inheritance to Charles V., and was transmitted by him with the crown of Spain to his son, Philip II. Charles himself was born at Ghent, the city whose revolt in 1539, he provoked by his oppressive taxes, and afterwards so severely punished. The chief provinces of the Netherlands were the Duchies of Brabant, Guelderland, Leinburg, and Luxemburg, and the countships of Holland, Zealand, Zutphen, Namur, and Flanders. The whole number of provinces was seventeen.—*Motley's Dutch Republic, Vol.* 1.

Philip II. appointed Margaret of Parma, regent of the Netherlands, and retired to Spain. He left with her the
1559. Cardinal Granvelle who was the real ruler. His rule was arbitrary and oppressive, and kindled great discontents. —*Motley's Dutch Republic, Vol.* 1.

The discontents increased, and 400 of the nobles signed and presented to Margaret the "compromise," a league to
1566. resist the Spanish Inquisition, which Philip was seeking to introduce. A courtier called the procession of nobles, a company of beggars. The name, which was given in derision, was at once adopted, and became the rallying-word of the patriots.—*Dutch Republic, Vol.* 1. *Philip II., Vol.* 1, *p.* 598.

Philip finally sent Duke Alva, who was a great general, but a cold-blooded tyrant, to rule as regent in the Netherlands.
1567. "His Council of Blood," and endless executions, have made his name infamous.—*Dutch Rep., Vol.* 2, *p.* 100.

William, Prince of Orange, taking early alarm, withdrew to his government of Holland, and raised the standard of
1568. revolt. Through his statesmanship and high character he finally secured a union of several of the provinces, and kept up the spirit of resistance to Spanish tyranny.—*Dutch Rep., Vol.* 2. *Philip II., Vol.* 2.

Alva imposed a tax of a tenth of the price of every article sold in the country, and required this to be paid at each
1569. successive sale. This enormous impost roused extensive revolts, and over 8,000 of the skilled workmen of the Netherlands fled to England, carrying many of the arts and manufactures of their country.—*Dutch Rep., Vol.* 2.

Some of the Netherland patriots, bearing the name of Water Beggars, made a maritime attack on the city of Brill,
1572. which speedily surrendered. This timely and important conquest greatly aided the patriots.—*Dutch Rep., Vol.* 2, *p.* 352.

After a bloody reign of six years, during which he had caused the execution of 18,600 persons, and slain in battles,
1573. sieges, and by starvation countless multitudes, the terrible Alva was removed, and Don Louis de Requesens sent to succeed him.—*Motley's Dutch Rep., Vol.* 2, *p.* 496.

After the death of Requesens, Don John of Austria, the Victor of Lepanto, and a half brother of Philip II., was
1576. appointed Governor of the Netherlands. The country he came to govern was in the agonies of its great struggle for liberty and bleeding at every pore. Don John died in 1578, and was succeeded by Alexander of Parma.—*Dutch Rep., Vol.* 3, *Chaps.* 4 *and* 5.

After many battles, sieges, and heroic deeds, William of Orange succeeded in effecting a union of the seven
1579. northern provinces of the Netherlands, to defend each other "with life, goods, and blood," and to maintain liberty. This Union of Utrecht, as it was called from the city where it was formed, embraced Guelderland, Holland, Zealand, Utrecht, Ghent, Overyssel, and Groningen. It formed the germ of the Netherland Republic, and was the prototype of the union of our American States, effected nearly 300 years later.—*Dutch Rep., Vol.* 3, *pp.* 410–417. *Modern Europe, Vol.* 1, *Let.* 69.

On the 26th of July the United Provinces issued their formal Declaration of Independence. William, Prince of
1581. Orange, was elected Stadtholder of Holland and Zealand, and the French Duke of Anjou chief of the other provinces.—*Dutch Rep., Vol.* 3, *p.* 504.

The repeated attempts made by the hirelings of Spain to assassinate the Prince of Orange, at length succeeded.
1584. On the 10th day of July, a wretch hired with Spanish gold, shot this great and good ruler, and William the Silent fell, as our own Lincoln fell, a martyr to the cause of his country.—*Dutch Rep., Vol.* 3, *p.* 609.

He was succeeded as Stadtholder by his son Maurice, then only 17 years old. In 1586 Maurice was chosen Stadtholder, and commander-in-chief of all the united provinces, and proved himself a worthy opponent of the Duke of Parma, the Spanish

Governor, who was still struggling to subdue the revolt.—*Mod. Europe, Vol.* 1, *Let.* 69. *Hume, Vol.* 4, *p.* 252. *Motley's United Netherlands, Vol.* 1, *p.* 17.

Maurice, assisted by English troops, surprised and captured Breda, and in the following years, took several other
1590. cities, after some of the most famous sieges in history.—*Mod. Europe, Vol.* 1, *Let.* 70. *Maurice in Am. Cy.*

The Dutch now steadily gained in power, and their fleets began to prey upon the commerce and distant posses-
1595. sions of Spain. Thus was laid the foundations of the long continued maritime supremacy of Holland.

ITALY.

Italy, at the beginning of the sixteenth century, was mainly divided between the Republic of Venice, then at the height of its power; the Duchy of Milan, which, with Lombardy and the Republics of Genoa and Florence, had just fallen into the hands of the French king; the Papal States, at that time under the infamous Pope Alexander VI., who, with the aid of his still more infamous son, Cæsar Borgia, had greatly increased the Papal power; and the kingdom of Naples and Sicily, then under Frederick III., but claimed by both France and Spain, which powers in November 1500, had concluded a treaty for its seizure and partition between them. Florence, under the De Medici, was the centre of the revived learning, and the arts and sciences were bursting forth with new splendors.

Naples was invaded by the French and Spanish armies, and Frederick III. resigned the throne he could no longer
1501. defend. During the next two years the Spanish General Gonsalvo de Cordova succeeded in expelling the French, and the crown of Naples was worn by Spanish kings from this time till 1713.—*Ferdinand and Isabella, Vol.* 3.

Pope Julius II., who was more soldier than saint, ascended the Papal throne. The principal events of his reign
1503. were the League of Cambray, 1508, by which he re-

covered some of his territories from the humbled Venetians; and the Holy League, 1511, which he organized to expel the French from Italy. He laid the foundation stone of St. Peter's Church in Rome.—*Pope Julius II. in Am. Cy.*

The battle of Ravenna, fought in 1512, has already been noticed under France.

Leo X., son of Lorenzo de Medici, the Magnificent, a Cardinal at 13, became Pope at 38 years of age. His reign
1513. was a brilliant era of arts and sciences, and he was greatly admired by his people. His sale of indulgencies, to obtain funds to support his magnificence and to build St. Peter's, was the immediate cause of the Reformation.—*Leo in Am. Cy.*

The battle of Marignano, fought September 13th and 14th, between the Swiss mercenaries in pay of the Duke of
1515. Milan, and the French troops under Francis I., gave the Duchy of Milan once more to France.

The Reformation gave a new turn to Papal history, compelling the Popes to shape their policy to new and defen-
1517. sive ends. Rome began to decline from her more than imperial power.

Raphael, the great Italian painter, died at Rome, April 6, at the age of 37 years. He was perhaps the greatest
1520. painter of modern times, and with his great contemporary, Michael Angelo, gave a wonderful impulse to the fine arts.—*Raphael in Am. Cy.*

Clement VII. was elected Pope. He belonged to the family of the Medici, and used all his power for the aggran-
1523. dizement of that family. He was the bitter opponent of the Reformation.

The defeat of the French at the battle of Pavia gave Milan and Northern Italy to the Emperor, Charles V., and ex-
1525. cluded the French from Italy for a long period, though French armies occasionally invaded Italian territory.

Clement VII., with the aid of the Emperor, suppressed the Republican government of Florence, and establishing the
1532. Duchy of Tuscany on its ruins, made his reputed son, Alexander De Medici, Duke. He was assassinated in 1536,

and succeeded by Cosmo De Medici, who afterwards assumed the title of Grand Duke Cosmo I.—*Medici in Am. Cy.*

Ignatius Loyola, a Spanish soldier, inspired by reading the
lives of the Catholic saints with a desire to do something
1534. for religion, founded, with six others, the society of
Jesus, or the Jesuits. These seven young men, students of the University of Paris, took their vows at Montmartre, near Paris, the 15th day of August.—*Loyola in American Cyclopedia.*

The order of the Jesuits was confirmed by Pope Paul III.
Thus arose a society destined to be the most powerful foe
1540. of the reformation, and one of the most remarkable and
powerful human organizations which ever existed on the earth. The order spread with unparalleled rapidity.—*Jesuits in Am. Cy.*

John Calvin, one of the greatest of the French reformers, after having been driven from several cities, Geneva,
1541. among the rest, was re-called to that city, which he
organized as a Christian community. It soon became the most moral town in Europe.—*Calvin in Am. Cy.*

The Council of Trent, the nineteenth and last great general
council of the church, was called on the occasion of the
1545. appeal of Luther from the decision of the Pope to a
council. It held several sessions with long recesses between them, and was finally dissolved in 1563. Its decrees fully defined the positions of the Papacy, and, taking clear issue with the reformed doctrines, made the breach wider and more hopeless between the parties.—*Council of Trent in Am. Cy.*

Michael Angelo, the great master of painting, sculpture, and
architecture, died at Rome, September 17, at the ad-
1563. vanced age of 89 years. He was to a large extent the
architect of St. Peter's. His great paintings are of world-wide renown.—*Angelo in Am. Cy.*

Galileo Galilei was born at Pisa, in Tuscany, February 15,
and died January 8, 1642. He was a great mechanist
1564. and mathematician, and made many most important
discoveries in physical science. He adopted the Copernican system, and was imprisoned for maintaining that the earth revolved.—*Galileo in Am. Cy.*

Pope Gregory XIII. signalized his reign by the reformation
1572. of the Calendar, which he effected in 1582. The New Style, as it is called, was not generally adopted till near a century later.

NORTHERN AND EASTERN EUROPE.

THE Northern nations, Norway, Sweden, and Denmark, and also Russia, bore but a subordinate part in the affairs of the sixteenth century. The Turks, who had gained a foothold in Europe, in the previous century, vigorously prosecuted their schemes of conquest during this. Their immense armies repeatedly advanced to the very heart of Europe, while their fleets kept the countries lying near the Mediterranean in perpetual alarm.

Selim I., "the ferocious," who had dethroned and put to
1520. death his father and all his brothers, died in 1520, and was succeeded by his son Solyman II., the Magnificent, a prince of splendid abilities and enterprising character.—*Chas. V., Vl.* 1, *p.* 523. *Lam. Hist. of Turkey, Vl.* 2, *p.* 291.

Gustavus Vasa, having successfully led the revolt of the
1523. Swedes against Christian II. of Denmark, was elected king. Thus was dissolved the union of Calmar, under which Sweden, Norway, and Denmark had been united for over a hundred years.—*Sweden in Am. Cy.*

Solyman invaded Hungary with an army of 300,000 men,
1526. gained the great victory of Mohacz, in which upwards of 20,000 Hungarians fell, overran the whole country, and carried near 200,000 persons into captivity.—*Charles V., Vol.* 2, *p.* 162. *Lamartine's Turkey, Vol.* 2, *p.* 314.

Solyman marched with 200,000 men to besiege Vienna, the
1529. capital of Ferdinand, Arch-Duke of Austria, who had been elected King of Hungary. After losing 20,000 men, the Turks retired without capturing the city.—*Lamartine's Turkey, Vol.* 2, *p.* 321.

Francis I., failing to gain allies among the Christian nations,
formed an alliance with Solyman, who engaged to in-
1536. vade Naples and attack Ferdinand in Hungary. These
engagements were faithfully performed in 1537, and the Turks gained a great victory over the Germans at Esseck.—*Charles V., Vol. 2, p.* 307.

Solyman II. died on the 5th of September, while engaged in
a campaign on the Danube in Hungary. He was suc-
1566. ceeded by his son, Selim II. The Turkish power began
to decline from this time.—*Lamartine's Turkey, Vol.* 2, *p.* 372.

It did not, however, go down without first adding to the tremendous crimes against humanity which had so often marked its career. The conquest of Cyprus, effected in this century, chills the blood by its enormous cruelties.—*Lamartine's Turkey, Vol.* 3.

Cyprus fell in November, 1570. The battle of Lepanto, described under Spain, avenged its fall, but did not recover
1571. it. The Turks kept their conquest, and rebuilt their
fleet.—*Lamartine's Turkey, Vol.* 3, *pp.* 46–50.

GENERAL VIEW

OF THE

SEVENTEENTH CENTURY.

The Seventeenth Century was a century of reactions. In both government and religion there was a retrograde movement. It was as if the advancing tides of freedom and of faith, urged too rapidly onward, had recoiled, and now crept backward on their path. In their haste, men had mingled too largely of evil with their good, and of falsehood with their truth, and their work perished.

The Reformation had triumphed in Germany, England, Scotland, Poland, and Sweden, and had successfully resisted the Spanish power in the Netherlands. In France, it had extorted toleration, and the Edict of Nantes; and only in Spain, had the Inquisition succeeded in crushing out the reform.

But Protestantism, in the very hour of its triumph, began to sink into a formalism, as lifeless and barren as that against which it had rebelled; and split into factions, which opposed each other more bitterly than they opposed Rome. The disciples of Luther detested the followers of Calvin, and many minor sects still further divided the forces of the Reformation. The reformers sought the corrupting alliances of the State, and religion was made subordinate to politics. The Jesuits, grown to immense power and wealth, borrowed the preaching and teaching arts of their Protestant foes, and rallied Catholic Europe for one final conflict to restore the sway of the Pope. The Thirty Years' war, the result of Jesuit teachings, quenched in blood these last hopes of the Papacy. But the increasing divisions of Christians left an open door for the incoming of the dark spirit of scepticism, which almost conquered Christendom at the close of this, and during the next, century.

In government, the same reactionary movement was seen. The wild sallies for liberty in Germany, and the grand and successful battle for republican freedom in the Netherlands, the popular constitutional government of Queen Elizabeth in England, and the triumphs of the popular party in France, were strangely enough followed by the despotic reigns of the Stuarts in Great Britain, the intensified absolutism of Richelieu and Louis Fourteenth in France, and the relentless tyranny of the Hapsburgs in Germany and Spain. The rising sun of liberty was totally eclipsed, and despotism reigned in unbroken night.

Once, at the middle of the century,—its midnight hour,—the spirit of revolt was aroused. The civil war in England, and the Fronde in France, shook for a brief spell the tyrants from their thrones. But the darkness, as if broken only by the lightnings of a passing tempest, speedily settled down again, and new despots succeeded the old. Only at the close of the century did England arise and throw off the yoke which France continued to wear a hundred years longer.

As to the remainder of Europe, petty wars filled the scene, and the lesser monarchs aped the pomp and the tyranny of Versailles. The Turks, wasted by Asiatic wars, and weakened by the inbred vices of their political system, ceased to disturb the rest of Europe. Just as the century was closing, the Russians were led by their great monarch, Peter I., into the ring of European powers, and Sweden flamed up into sudden glory under her warrior-king, Charles the Twelfth.

In America alone the century was one of progress. The destined State-builders of the new world, educated in the stormy trials and triumphs of the sixteenth century, were now driven forth by the iron despotism of the seventeenth; and the long known but hitherto unbroken wilds of America were everywhere suddenly filled with teeming colonies. It was as if God, having ripened the seeds for this new world, had now permitted them to be roughly shaken from the European tree.

The intellectual movement of the century was one of great and splendid progress. Bacon's writings led the way; and Descartes and Locke in philosophy, Galileo and Newton in physical science, and Milton and Racine in literature, with many others, pushed the new learning of the world far beyond the boundaries of ancient thought, and paved the way for the grander triumphs of our own age.

Such were the main features of this somewhat singular period, —a century apparently out of place,—a return of darkness after the day-dawn.

AMERICA.

American history during the sixteenth century had been the history of explorations and adventures, in a remote and wilderness continent. When the seventeenth century opened, it remained almost as unbroken a wilderness as Columbus found it. At distant points, a few settlements, chiefly of a commercial character, existed, and no one seems to have suspected that here was the future home of great States. But the struggles of Europe had been preparing many liberty-loving souls, and the reactions of the seventeenth century now drove them forth to enjoy in the new world the freedom denied them in the old. Commercial companies on a gigantic scale, with powers of colonization and government, had begun to come into vogue, and the work of settlement was ready to begin. Raleigh's plans had failed, but they had paved the way for more successful efforts.

1602. Bartholomew Gosnold, with the concurrence of Raleigh, sailed to the New England coast, discovered Cape Cod, and attempted to plant a settlement on Elizabeth Island in Buzzard's Bay; but the settlers, fearing the Indians and famine, re-embarked.—*Bancroft, Vol.* 1, *p.* 112.

1606. The favorable accounts brought to England by Raleigh, Gosnold, and others, at length, produced definite desires to colonize the new continent, and James I. granted charters to two companies organized for trade, settlement, and government—the London and the Plymouth companies.—*Bancroft, Vol.* 1, *p.* 120.

1607. Three ships bearing 105 men were sent forth by the London Company, under Captain Newport, to plant a colony in Virginia. In April they sailed up the James River, named after their king, and in May they landed and established their colony at Jamestown.—*Bancroft, Vol.* 1, *p.* 125.

1608. Captain John Smith, one of the colonists, and a man of much experience and courage, was captured by the Indians while exploring the Chickahominy River, a stream now celebrated for McClellan's campaign, and would have been put to death but for the interference of Pocahontas, the daughter of the Indian king Powhatan.—*Bancroft, Vol.* 1, *p.* 130.

While the English settlers were clearing their fields in Jamestown, another colony was building its few cabins far to the north. Champlain led forth some French settlers and founded Quebec.—*Bancroft, Vol.* 1, *p.* 28.

This same year, some of the Puritans of England, the future settlers of New England, fled from their native land and sought shelter and freedom in Holland.—*Bancroft, Vol.* 1, *p.* 301.

1609. Henry Hudson, sent out by the Dutch East India Company to discover a western passage to Asia, explored the coast from Baffin's Bay, and finally sailed up the beautiful river that now bears his name.—*Bancroft, Vol.* 2, *p.* 265.

1614. Holland, claiming the territory discovered by Hudson, sent forth trading parties to traffic with the Indians, and a fort on Manhattan, now New York, Island was the germ of the greatest city of the western continent.—*Bancroft, Vol.* 2, *p.* 272.

1619. After a succession of hardships and troubles, and also of governors, Gov. Yeardley was appointed Captain General to succeed the tyrant Argall, and in June he summoned the first colonial assembly that ever met in Virginia. This was the first instance of representative government on this continent.—*Bancroft, Vol.* 1, *p.* 153.

1620. The English Puritans in Holland at length determined to find a home in America, and having obtained a patent from the London Company, one hundred of them came over in the Mayflower and landed, after many hardships, at Plymouth, in Massachusetts Bay, the 22nd day of December. This was the germ of the old Bay State.—*Bancroft, Vol.* 1, *p.* 313. *Lossing, p.* 78.

The same year that the Pilgrims came to Plymouth, a Dutch man-of-war landed at Jamestown, in Virginia, twenty negroes who were sold as slaves.—*Bancroft, Vol.* 1, *p.* 176.

The growth of the white man's settlements in Virginia
awakened the jealousy and hatred of the Indians; and,
1622. forming an extensive conspiracy, they attempted to ex-
terminate the settlers at a single blow. In one hour 347 persons were cut off, and the massacre would have been general but for the warning given by a friendly Indian.—*Bancroft, Vol.* 1. *p.* 182.

The territory of New Hampshire was early granted to two enterprising men, Ferdinand Gorges and John Mason; and,
1623. under the auspices of a company formed by them, a
settlement was made at two places near Portsmouth and Dover. *Lossing's United States, p.* 79. *Bancroft, Vol.* 1, *p.* 328.

The earliest settlement in Delaware was made by a Dutch
company under De Vries, who sailed December 12th,
1630. and established themselves near Lewiston. This colony
perished by the hands of the Indians within a few months of the time it was planted. The Swedes, under the lead of their great king Gustavus Adolphus, planned colonies as early as 1624. Their first colony was established in 1638 at New Castle.—*Lossing, p.* 92. *Bancroft, Vol.* 2, *pp.* 281–287.

While De Vries was making ready to leave Holland with his thirty colonists for Delaware, Gov. John Winthrop was already landed at Salem, Mass. with a large reinforcement of settlers, numbering, according to Lossing, 300 families; according to others, 500 souls. Others followed, and during the summer founded Boston.—*Bancroft, Vol.* 1, *pp.* 354–356. *Lossing, p.* 118.

Connecticut was first settled by colonists from New Plymouth,
who built a trading house at Windsor. The Dutch, who
1633. also claimed the territory, built a fort at Hartford the
same year before the English arrived. Other settlers made their way through the wilderness from Massachusetts Bay, and

in 1636 the Rev. Thomas Hooker, with some fellow-pastors and their congregations, emigrated from the vicinity of Boston and settled at Hartford and other points.—*Lossing, p.* 86. *Bancroft, Vol.* 1, *pp.* 395–396.

The despotism that drove out the Puritans to Holland and
New England also oppressed the Catholics, and led
1634. George Calvert, Lord Baltimore, to plan a colony in
America as a refuge for his Catholic brethren. In March a company of them arrived and settled at St. Mary's.—*Bancroft, Vol.* 1, *p.* 246. *Lossing, p.* 82.

Roger Williams, a young minister, having, in advance of the
age, adopted the doctrines of freedom of conscience and
1636. religious toleration, was exiled from Massachussetts;
and, after passing the winter among the friendly Indians, he came, in the spring of 1636, with five friends, to a place which they called Providence, and began the settlement of Rhode Island.—*Bancroft, Vol.* 1, *pp.* 377–379.

The spread of the English settlements through the hunting
grounds of the Indians awakened the natural jealousy of
1637. the red men, and the Pequods, a tribe living in eastern
Connecticut, opened hostilities. After several murders and outrages committed by them, the settlers raised a military force, which, defeating the Indians, drove them from their hiding places and finally from the State.—*Bancroft, Vol.* 1, *pp.* 398–401.

The same year with the Pequod war, Harvard College was founded. The next year, John Harvard bequeathed to the infant college his library and half of his estate. This was the first American college.—*Bancroft, Vol.* 1, *p.* 459.

The time of the settlement of North Carolina is not well
known. Settlers from Virginia early made their way into
1640. the regions now belonging to North Carolina and settled
there. Perhaps even before 1640 there were settlements begun.

The New England colonies, now numbering more than 20,000
people, impelled by their fear of the Dutch and of the
1643. Indians, formed the first American Union.—*Bancroft,*
Vol. 1, *p.* 420.

Rev. John Eliot, full of pity for the heathen condition of the

Indians, learned their language, and about this date
1646. began preaching to them in their own tongue.

After the English Parliament had beheaded the king, it took early measures to secure the obedience of the American
1651. colonies. New England, which was in sympathy with the popular party in England, submitted at once. Virginia was full of royalists, who now banished Puritans from the colony, and openly acknowledged the son of the beheaded king as Charles II. A powerful fleet was sent against them, but a submission was finally purchased without bloodshed by the grant of large political privileges to the rebellious colonists.—*Bancroft, Vol.* 1, *p.* 211. *Lossing. p.* 108.

Eliot translated and published the Bible in the Indian language. Eliot's noble Christian labors in behalf of the
1663. poor natives are in beautiful contrast with the treatment they ordinarily received. He induced large numbers of them to give up their savage customs, and to live in civilized communities; and he lived to see twenty-four of them become preachers of the gospel to their own tribes.—*Eliot in Am. Cy.*

The heartless and extravagant Charles II., having reached the throne, recklessly gave away to his brother, James,
1664. Duke of York, the Dutch colony of New Netherlands. A fleet was sent out by the Duke to secure his new possessions, and, on the 3d of September, Manhattan was surrendered by Gov. Stuyvesant, and its name changed to New York.—*Bancroft, Vol.* 2, *p.* 314. *Lossing, p.* 144.

The same fleet brought over Royal Commissioners with instructions to inquire into the affairs of the colonies, with the secret intent to deprive them of their Charters, and bring them under the immediate control of the Crown. English tyranny began its encroachments, and America began its resistance.—*Bancroft, Vol.* 2, *p.* 78.

The French Jesuit missionaries, James Marquette and Claude Dablon, established a mission station at St. Mary's. This
1668. was the oldest settlement of Europeans in Michigan.—*Bancroft, Vol.* 3, *p.* 152.

South Carolina was first settled by the English, in 1670, at

1670. Beaufort. This place they abandoned for a position above Charleston on the Ashley River, This also was forsaken, and in 1680 they founded Charleston.—*Lossing, p.* 98. *Bancroft Vol.* 2, *p.* 169.

Virginia was granted by Charles II., without any regard to the
1673. wishes of the colonists, to Lord Culpepper and the Earl of Arlington. So little did English monarchs respect American rights.—*Bancroft, Vol.* 2, *p.* 209.

The steady growth of the New England colonies encroached
1675. upon the Indian territories and awakened a spirit of resentment. Philip of Pokanoket, chief of the Wampanoags, having been subjected to some personal affronts, took up arms and began hostilities. Other tribes joined him, and Indians lay in ambush around all the frontier settlements. Many settlers were shot in their fields. Deerfield was burned, and Hadley was saved only by Goffe, the regicide. Several other towns fell the next year, but the Indians were finally subdued and King Philip killed. More than 600 white men fell in the field, and as many as 600 houses were burned. It was a terrible war for the young colonies, and as oppressive in its burdens as the Revolutionary War, which it preceded just one hundred years.—*Bancroft, Vol.* 2, *pp.* 100–109. *Lossing, p.* 124.

Indian wars also raged in Virginia, and Gov. Berkeley having
1676. refused permission to the people to organize and arm a force for their defence, a rebellion broke out under the lead of Nathaniel Bacon. The rebels triumphed and extorted large concessions of popular liberty. War ensued, Jamestown was burned by Bacon to save it from falling into the hands of the royalists. The revolution was nearly complete when Bacon died, October 1, and the rebellion speedily ended. It was a hundred years too early.—*Bancroft, Vol.* 2, *pp.* 217–229.

La Salle and Hennepin, two Frenchmen, built and fitted out
1679. a vessel at Niagara, and, sailing through Lake Erie, navigated and named Lake St. Clair, planted a trading house at Mackinaw, and cast anchor in Green Bay. They went thence in canoes to the head of Lake Michigan and entered St. Joseph's River, in Michigan.—*Bancroft, Vol.* 3, *p.* 164.

William Penn, a Quaker, having obtained from Charles II. 1682. a grant of the present State of Pennsylvania, established settlements, and, in 1683, founded Philadelphia. He constructed his government on the most enlightened principles of liberty and religious toleration. His wise and just treatment of the Indians gave his colony total exemption from Indian wars for many years.—*Bancroft, Vol.* 2, *p.* 362–387.

This same year, La Salle, the French discoverer, leaving Illinois, sailed down the Mississippi River. He named the country on its banks Louisiana in honor of his sovereign, and claimed the territory for France.—*Bancroft, Vol.* 3, *p.* 168.

1686. James II., seeking to consolidate all the northern colonies, sent over Sir Edmund Andros, who had before been Governor of New York and New Jersey, as Governor of all New England. He ruled with the greatest tyranny and sowed seeds of after revolutions.—*Bancroft, Vol.* 12, *p.* 425.

1687. Andros, having established his authority in Massachusetts and Rhode Island, came to Connecticut and demanded the surrender of its charter; but the charter was snatched from the table of the Assembly which was discussing the question of surrendering it, and hidden in an old hollow oak, known ever afterwards as the Charter Oak.—*Bancroft, Vol.* 2, *p.* 430.

When James was driven from his throne in 1688, the people seized Andros, and sent him and fifty of his associates to England.—*Bancroft, Vol.* 2, *p.* 446.

1689. The accession of William III. brought a war with France, and, as a consequence, a war between the French and the English colonies, known as King William's war. It was fought mostly on the frontiers, and with the aid of the Indians.—*Bancroft, Vol.* 3, *pp.* 175–185. *Lossing, p.* 131.

1690. Common danger led to a union of the colonies for mutual defence, and an "American Congress" was called at Albany.—*Bancroft, Vol.* 3, *p.* 183.

In January of the same year a party of French and Indians left Montreal, and, making their way through the wilderness, attacked and burned Schenectady. February 8th, another party captured and burned Salmon Falls, New Hampshire.—*Bancroft, Vol.* 3, *p.* 182.

The war closed with the peace of Ryswick in 1697.

An excitement on the subject of witchcraft broke out at
1692. Salem, Massachusetts. Hundreds of persons were arrested and imprisoned, and some were put to death.—*Lossing, p.* 132. *Bancroft, Vol.* 3, *p.* 75.

ENGLAND AND SCOTLAND.

The long and brilliant reign of Elizabeth, the last of the Tudors, reached a little beyond the sixteenth century. The seventeenth was the century of the Stuarts, as narrow-minded, heartless, and tyrannical a set of rulers as ever disgraced a throne. England and Scotland having been united by the accession of the Stuarts, who were hereditary monarchs of both kingdoms, the old-time border wars and forays between these kingdoms ceased, except as they sometimes took opposite sides in the civil wars. The century was a stirring and momentous one in English history. Two great revolutions and civil wars sprung from the irrepressible conflicts between kingly despotism and popular liberty. The general result was in favor of freedom, and the absolute tyranny of the Stuarts may therefore be counted to have done more for English liberty, than the more constitutional reigns of the Tudors.

On the death of Elizabeth, James VI. of Scotland, son of the un-
1603. fortunate Mary, Queen of Scots, succeeded to the throne as the next heir, and took the title of James I. He was the first of the House of Stuart who sat on the English throne. An awkward, pedantic, and obstinate Scotchman, he was a devout believer in the divine right of kings, and his extravagant abuse of his royal prerogatives laid the foundation of the misfortunes of his children and his country.—*Hume, Vol.* 4, *pp.* 378, 494.

The Roman Catholics, enraged by James' unexpected intol-

1605. erance, plotted the destruction of the entire royal family and the two Houses of the English Parliament. The Gunpowder Plot, as it was called, aimed to blow up the Parliament house when both the Lords and Commons were assembled to hear the king's speech. It was discovered just in time to prevent the catastrophe, which would perhaps have changed the history of England for centuries.—*Hume, Vol.* 4, *pp.* 400–405.

John Milton, the greatest of modern epic poets, was born in
1608. London the 9th day of December. His sublime poetry, and no less masterly prose, constituted an era in English literature. He took the side of the Republicans in the Civil War, and as Cromwell's Secretary for Foreign Affairs, he contributed much to the dignity and strength of the Commonwealth. —*Milton in Am. Cy.*

James' daughter, Elizabeth, was married to Frederic V., Elec-
1613. tor of the Palatinate, and afterwards the unfortunate leader in the first period of the Thirty Years' War. A hundred and one years later, her grandson, George I., came to the throne as founder of a new dynasty of English kings.—*Hume, Vol.* 4, *p.* 426.

Francis Bacon, the greatest thinker of his times, was made
1618. Lord High Chancellor, and two years later he gave to the world his greatest work, the *Novum Organum*, which he had written twelve times.—*Bacon in Am. Cy.*

The same year with Bacon's exaltation, Sir Walter Raleigh, whose name had been linked so intimately with the colonization of America, was beheaded, after having suffered thirteen years' imprisonment. His fate was universally deplored as an act of meanness and weakness on the part of James.—*Hume, Vol.* 4, *p.* 452.

A marriage having been planned between James' son, Charles,
1623. Prince of Wales, and the daughter of Philip IV. of Spain, Buckingham, the worthless and insolent favorite of the king, proposed to the young prince the romantic project of a private journey to Spain to visit his future bride. The visit was accordingly made, but the match was afterwards broken off, and much ill will grew out of it.—*Hume, Vol.* 4, *pp.* 475–482.

Charles I. succeeded to the throne on the death of his father.
1625. He was a much abler and more excellent man than James, but entertained the same extravagant notions of his royal prerogatives, and was even more crooked and insincere in his conduct. His reign was one long battle with his subjects, in which he finally suffered defeat and death.—*Macaulay's England, Vol.* 1, *p.* 64.

Soon after the accession of Charles, he completed his marriage engagement with Henrietta, daughter of Louis XIII. of France, a Catholic princess, who succeeded in tincturing the minds of her sons with her own faith.—*Hume, Vol.* 5, *p.* 1. *Knight's Pictorial England, Vol.* 3, *p.* 109.

The struggle between Charles and his Parliament ran so high,
1629. that he at length arrested several members and sent them to prison. This creating an immense excitement, he dismissed Parliament, and attempted, for the next eleven years, to rule without a Parliament.—*Hume, Vol.* 3, *p.* 59. *Pictorial England, Vol.* 3, *p.* 142.

Thomas Wentworth, a member of Parliament, whom the king
1633. had won from the opposition by making him Earl of Strafford and by other favors, was appointed Lord Deputy of Ireland and called an Irish Parliament, which he browbeat, and finally made the king's power absolute in that part of the realm.—*Pictorial Eng., Vol.* 3, *p.* 169. *Macaulay, Vol.* 1, *p.* 68.

Charles, who was attempting arbitrarily to rule without a Par-
1634. liament, now levied ship-money, a tax for the support of the navy. The tax created great excitement, and the celebrated John Hampden, resisting its payment, was tried and condemned.—*Pictorial Eng., Vol.* 3, *p.* 179. *Macaulay, Vol.* 1, *p.* 70.

Archbishop Laud, another tool of the king's tyranny, prepared,
1638. in 1637, a liturgy which he and his master attempted to force on the Scotch Presbyterians, who, in the following year, 1638, formed and subscribed to the National Covenant, and raised riots which speedily grew into rebellion.—*Pictorial Eng., Vol.* 3, *pp.* 186–187. *Macaulay, Vol.* 1, *p.* 73.

The Covenanters assembled in great force under their gene-

1639. ral Leslie, seized Edinburgh and other places, and advanced into England. Charles was compelled at length to call another Parliament, after ruling eleven years without one. *Pictorial Eng., Vol.* 3, *pp.* 203–204.

After calling, April 13th, and dissolving, May 5th, a Parliament, which he found determined to assert the liberties
1640. of the people, Charles was compelled, by the war in Scotland and the demands of his people, to assemble, Nov. 3, the celebrated Long Parliament, so called because of its long reign.—*Pictorial Eng., Vol.* 3, *pp.* 210–216–226. *Macaulay, Vol.* 1. *p.* 75.

The Long Parliament, which had from the outset exhibited its determination to resist the king, speedily ordered the
1641. arrest of Laud and Strafford, the chief advisers of his tyranny, and tried and convicted the latter of treason. Charles deserted his fallen minister, and Strafford was beheaded.—*Pictorial Eng., Vol.* 3, *pp.* 242–245. *Macaulay, Vol.* 1, *p.* 76.

The struggle between Charles and his Parliament at length resulted in the terrible civil war which overturned the
1642. throne, and finally sent the king himself to the block. The Parliament party were called "Roundheads" and the royalists, "Cavaliers." The first regular battle of the war was fought at Edgehill, October 23. This battle was followed by many others.—*Pictorial Eng., Vol.* 3, *p.* 297. *Hume, Vol.* 5, *p.* 236.

In the midst of these commotions Isaac Newton, the great physical philosopher, was born, December 25. He died March 20, 1727. His greatest discovery was that of the law of gravitation.—*Newton in Am. Cy.*

The battle of Marston Moor, won by the valor of Oliver Cromwell and his regiment of "Ironsides," gave a fatal blow
1644. to the king's cause. It was fought the 2d day of July.—*Pictorial Eng., Vol.* 3, *p.* 315. *Macaulay, Vol.* 1. *p.* 91.

The battle of Naseby was fought June 14, and resulted in a complete and crushing defeat of the king's army. It
1645. was followed by other victories of the "Roundheads." *Hume, Vol.* 5, *p.* 310.

Charles, defeated at every point, finally fled towards Scotland,

1646. and threw himself upon the protection of the Scotch army. The Scots, January 1647, sold him to Parliament for £400,000, which they claimed as arrears from England. —*Hume, Vol.* 5, *pp.* 323, 327, 328.

A period of strife between the Parliament in which Presbyterians predominated, and the Army in which the Independents had the control, ensued. The Independents, who were republicans, finally triumphed, and succeeded in getting Charles tried and condemned; and, January 30th, he was beheaded.—*Pictorial Eng., Vol.* 3. *Hume, Vol.* 5, *pp.* 366, 377.

1649.

After the king's death the House of Commons proceeded to abolish royalty, and a republican form of government was established under the name of the Commonwealth.—*Pictorial Eng., Vol.* 3, *p.* 399. *Macaulay, Vol.* 1, *p.* 100.

Ireland and Scotland refused to acknowledge the supremacy of the Parliament after the death of the king. Cromwell crossed over to Ireland, and, by the latter part of May, after a campaign of nine months, suppressed the rebellion.—*Hume, Vol.* 5, *p.* 398. *Pictorial Eng., Vol,* 3, *p.* 401.

1650.

Prince Charles, on the invitation of the Scots, passed over from the continent to Scotland, and was formally proclaimed as Charles II.—*Hume, Vol,* 5, *p.* 407. *Macaulay, Vol.* 1, *p.* 101.

Charles, after suffering a severe defeat at Dunbar, Aug. 1650, mustered a fresh army, and marched into England. Cromwell immediately pursued and gained another and decisive victory over him at Worcester. Charles fled to France, and never reappeared in England till his final restoration in 1660.—*Pictorial Eng., Vol.* 3, *p.* 405. *Hume, Vol.* 5. *p.* 417.

1651.

The several disputes between England and Holland finally resulted in a naval war, brought on by a collision between the English fleet, under the great sea-hero Blake, and the Dutch fleet, under the famous Van Tromp. Blake gained the victory in this and several subsequent battles, but finally suffered a severe reverse, and the victorious Tromp fixed a broom at his mast-head to signify his intention to sweep the seas, of English vessels.—*Hume, Vol.* 5, *pp.* 428–431.

1652.

Cromwell finally dispersed the remnant of the Long Parlia-

1653. ment, known as the "Rump," and assembled a new one called from one of its members, named Praise God Barebone, the "Barebone's Parliament." This also proving unfriendly to his policy, he dismissed it, and, with the advice and concurrence of his principal officers, assumed, December 16th, supreme power under the title of Lord Protector of England, Scotland, and Ireland—*Pictorial Eng.*, *Vol.* 3, *pp.* 410–413. *Macaulay*, *Vol.* 1, *pp.* 102–104.

The naval war with Holland was ended by the peace of West-
1654. minster, in which Cromwell obtained terms so favorable to England as greatly to strengthen his government.—*Hume*, *Vol.* 5, *p.* 447.

The Scotch again rebelled against the Commonwealth, and were subdued by General Monk, whom Cromwell sent against them.—*Pictorial Eng.*, *Vol.* 3, *p.* 416.

Cromwell united with France in a war against Spain, and sent
1655. out two fleets, one to the Mediterranean, and the other to the West Indies, to prey on the Spanish commerce. The West Indian fleet, though in the main unfortunate, made the important conquest of Jamaica, which has ever since remained in the hands of the English.—*Hume*, *Vol.* 5, *pp.* 459–462.

Blake attacked the Spanish plate fleet in the harbor of Santa
1656. Cruz, and compelled the Spaniards to abandon and burn their ships with all their treasure.—*Hume*, *Vol.* 5, *p.* 463.

Cromwell was solicited by many who wished to see the more
1657. stable forms of monarchy replace the military power, or who desired to flatter the Protector, to assume the title of King, but this sagacious ruler, fearing commotions among the Republicans, refused the empty title.—*Pictorial Eng.*, *Vol.* 3, *p.* 421.

On the 3d day of September, Cromwell died, having governed
1658. England with more of ability and success than any of her hereditary monarchs. By his directions, his son was proclaimed Lord Protector, as his successor.—*Macaulay*, *Vol.* 1, *p.* 108.

Before Cromwell's death, his soldiers, in conjunction with those of France, gained a splendid victory over the Spaniards, and took Dunkirk, which was delivered up to the English.—*Pictorial Eng., Vol.* 3, *p.* 427. *Hume, Vol.* 5, *p.* 480.

Richard Cromwell was a good man, but by no means equal to the exigency of the times. His father's military
1659. officers conspired against him, and on the 5th of May he voluntarily resigned his office. The Long Parliament was assembled by call of the army officers, and resumed the function of government.—*Hume, Vol.* 5, *pp.* 493–494.

General Monk and the army in Scotland declared against the Long Parliament, and marched in triumph to London.
1660. A new Parliament was elected which voted to recall the Stuarts, and accordingly Charles II. returned and mounted the throne of his ancestors.—*Hume, Vol.* 5, *pp.* 506–518. *Pictorial Eng., Vol,* 3, *p.* 432.

Sir Edward Hyde was created Earl of Clarendon, and made prime minister.—*Macaulay, Vol.* 1, *p.* 134.

Charles had learned nothing by his own exile, nor by his father's fate. An act of uniformity was passed, requiring
1662. every clergyman to be ordained by the Episcopal bishops, and to assent to the book of common prayer. Upwards of two thousand ministers were thrust out of their livings by this act, and great commotions were excited.—*Macaulay, Vol.* 1, *p.* 144. *Pictorial Eng., Vol.* 3, *p.* 691.

The king greatly increased the general discontent by his marriage with Catherine of Portugal, and by the sale of Dunkirk to the French monarch for £400,000.—*Macaulay, Vol.* 1, *pp.* 148, 149.

The superiority of the Dutch, in their commercial enterprises, excited the jealousy of the English, and led to another
1664. war between these powers.—*Macaulay, Vol.* 1, *p.* 149. *Pictorial Eng., Vol.* 3, *p.* 695.

The great Plague in London raged with such violence as to suspend all trade, and added to the popular gloom and
1665. discontent. Over 100,000 persons are said to have fallen victims to it.

While the plague was raging, the Duke of York met the Dutch fleet off Lowestoft, June 3d, and conquered them in a great battle, destroying eighteen ships and killing over 8,000 men.—*Pictorial Eng., Vol.* 3, *p.* 695. *Macaulay, Vol.* 1, *p.* 150.

The French having joined Holland in the war, an immense
1666. fleet of 76 ships was fitted out under Tromp and De Ruyter. They soon met the English fleet of 74 sail, and a terrible battle of four days ensued, which was finally decided in favor of the English, who had been reinforced during the engagement.—*Hume, Vol.* 6, *pp.* 46–48.

The great fire in London, which occurred this year, broke out the 3d of September and raged three days, destroying two thirds of the entire city.—*Pictorial Eng., Vol.* 3, *p.* 699. *Hume, Vol.* 6, *p.* 50.

The peace concluded at Breda at length closed this war
1667. between Holland and England, but not till the Dutch fleet had sailed up the Thames and burned several vessels.—*Hume, Vol.* 6, *p.* 54.

The threatening ambition of Louis XIV. induced England,
1668. Holland, and Sweden to form a triple alliance to curb the aggressions of France.—*Hume, Vol.* 6, *p.* 65.

Under the auspices of the triple alliance the peace of Aix la Chapelle was concluded, in which France and Spain concurred, and the tranquility of Europe seemed to be secured.—*Pictorial Eng., Vol.* 3, *p.* 706.

Clarendon, although a friend to constitutional liberty, fell
1670. under the popular disfavor in 1667, and was impeached and banished. After a variety of counsels, the Cabal Ministry was formed, and proved the most tyrannical and unscrupulous agent of royal prerogative.—*Hume, Vol.* 6, *p.* 82.

The Cabal being at length broken down, a new ministry was
1673. formed under the Earl of Danby, which lent all its influence to make the king's power absolute.—*Macaulay, Vol.* 1, *p.* 175.

The opponents of the Duke of York and the Papists finally secured the passage of the test act, which required every one holding civil office to partake of the Communion in the English Church.—*Hume, Vol.* 6, *p.* 117. *Macaulay, Vol.* 1, *p.* 173.

Charles, who was often a pensioner of Louis XIV., had taken

1674. part in that monarch's Holland war. He was now compelled by the popular voice to conclude a separate peace with the Dutch.—*Hume, Vol.* 6, *p*, 123. *Macaulay, Vol.* 1, *p.* 174.

Charles being childless, his brother, the Duke of York, a
1678. bigoted Papist, was heir to the throne. Great uneasiness was felt in view of this fact, and ready credence was given to a pretended Popish plot to murder the king. All England was in uproar, and stringent laws were made against the Papists.—*Macaulay, Vol.* 1, *pp.* 180–186. *Hume, Vol.* 6, *p.* 171.

The tide was setting again towards liberty, and Parliament
1679. passed the Habeas Corpus Act to defend citizens against illegal imprisonment. This is justly esteemed one of the great bulwarks of British liberty.—*Hume, Vol.* 6, *p.* 204. *Macaulay, Vol.* 1, *p.* 193.

The popular jealousy of the Duke of York at length reached such a pitch that Parliament introduced a bill for excluding him from the throne. Charles dissolved Parliament to prevent its passage, and the question became the great issue in English politics.—*Macaulay, Vol.* 1, *pp.* 193, 194.

A conspiracy of several English noblemen was formed to re-
1683. sist the accession of James, Duke of York, in case of his brother's death, and it is alleged a subordinate plan was concocted to assassinate Charles and establish a Commonwealth again. This latter plan is known as the Rye House Plot. Among those who fell victims to the king's rage on account of this plot, were two great statesmen and pure patriots, Lord William Russell and Algernon Sydney.—*Hume, Vol.* 6, *pp.* 263–272. *Macaulay, Vol.* 1, *pp.* 208, 209.

Charles II. died the 6th of February, and was succeeded by
1685. his brother, James II., a man of mean and tyrannical temper. The Earl of Rochester, brother to the Earl of Clarendon, was made prime minister.—*Macaulay, Vol.* 1, *pp.* 345–351.

The terms, Whig and Tory, had been used as nicknames of
1686. the two parties who respectively favored and opposed the exclusion of the Duke of York. Afterwards, the

Whigs became the party of popular liberty, and denied the divine right of kings ; the Tories were the supporters of kingly prerogative. Their contests were long and bitter.—*Macaulay, Vol.* 1, *p.* 200.

1688.

James II. proved one of the greatest tyrants that ever sat on England's throne. His reign was a succession of usurpations. He, at length, arrested and tried seven bishops for petitioning against one of his illegal commands. The bishops were acquitted amidst the tumultuous rejoicings of all London.

William of Orange, James' son-in-law, having been invited by the Whigs, landed at Torbay, in England, with 15,000 soldiers. James, frightened by the popular rage against him, fled to France. Thus was accomplished the great political revolution of '88.—*Macaulay, Vol.* 2. *Hume, Vol.* 6, *pp.* 323–349.

1689.

The Parliament invited William of Orange and his wife, Mary, jointly to accept the throne. They assented, and were accordingly proclaimed, February 13th, amidst great rejoicings.—*Macaulay, Vol.* 2, *pp.* 511–513.

1690.

Ireland took the side of the deposed king, and the Irish rushed to arms in immense numbers. James, accepting their invitation, went over in person to Ireland to place himself at the head of an insurrection in his favor. William finally went to lead the English forces. Both armies met at Boyne, the 1st of July, and after a tremendous conflict, the English came off victors. James fled again to France.—*Macaulay, Vol.* 3, *pp.* 498–508.

1691.

The war in Ireland continued till Limerick, after a second long and terrible siege, surrendered, October 1st, when the peace of Limerick was signed. Of the Irish soldiers, 10,000 or 12,000 went over to France, and became the famous Irish Brigade in the armies of Louis XIV.—*Pictorial Eng., Vol.* 4, *p.* 34. *Macaulay, Vol.* 4, *pp.* 84–88.

1692.

William's accession had united the fortunes of Holland and England, and almost necessarily involved England in the continential war which William was waging against the ambition of the great French king. James having fled to Louis for aid, additional cause of war existed against that monarch. The combined Dutch and English fleets met the French fleet near La Hogue, where a great army was embarking for the invasion of England. After a series of battles, lasting five days, the allies gained, May 24th, a great victory.—*Macaulay, Vol.* 4, *pp.* 189–192.

At the battle of Steinkirk, fought June 30th, the allies were severely beaten.—*Macaulay, Vol.* 4, *pp.* 223–225.

The war went on, and at Neerwinden, on the 19th of July,
more than a year after his defeat at Steinkirk, William
1693. was again beaten, though he fought with great personal
valor.—*Macaulay, Vol.* 4, *pp.* 324–328.

On the 28th of December, William's wife, the good queen
Mary, died. The loss was a severe one to husband and
1694. people. Her popularity had helped to save him from
the conspiracies which now again began to be formed against him by the Jacobites or friends ot James, and gave him but little repose the remainder of his reign.—*Macaulay, Vol.* 4, *p.* 424.

The city of Namur, which the French had taken by a siege in
1692, William now, after another and more terrible, re-
1695. took. The tide of French victories now turned, and the
fortunes of Louis began to wane.—*Macaulay, Vol.* 4, *pp.* 468–477.

On the 20th of September was concluded the peace of Ryswick, between France, England, Holland, and Spain,
1697. and the long and bloody war closed. France acknow-
ledged William as king of England, and abandoned the cause of James.—*Macaulay, Vol.* 4, *p.* 639.

FRANCE.

The opening of the Seventeenth Century found France, under the rule of the brilliant Henry IV. and his great minister Sully, rapidly recovering from the disorders and debts occasioned by the long religious wars of the preceding century. Henry and Sully were really profound statesman, and their plans for the adjustment of European affairs, and the promotion of the general peace, were far-reaching and sagacious. To them has been attributed the first conception of that great object of modern European politics, the Balance of powers. But France was not to escape so lightly the effects of that terrible crime of her rulers, the murder of her best citizens, in the St. Bartholomew massacre.

During this century, the French monarchy was the leading power of Europe; but her lead tended towards despotism the most complete and unyielding the world has ever seen.—*White's France.*

On the 14th of May, as Henry was about to place himself at
the head of the Protestant forces in the last great con-
1610. test just opening between the rival religions, an assassin
pressed to his carriage window, and, with the blow of a dagger, destroyed the foremost man of the age. Henry was succeeded by his son Louis XIII., a boy of nine years. The queen mother, the unprincipled and unfortunate Mary de Medici, was appointed Regent. The nobles, no longer held in check, burst forth into all their old turbulence, and Sully retired in disgust.—*White's France, pp.* 306–309.

The disorders compelled the Regent to summon the States
General, the great council of the French nobility and
1614. clergy. After a few months of useless dispute, the as-
sembly was dissolved. It was the last meeting till the stormy days of the Revolution, nearly two hundred years later.—*White's France, p.* 310.

There had appeared among the delegates to the States Gene-

ral, a pale young priest of remarkable ability, who after-
1624. wards entered the service of the queen-regent. His talent for command soon made him master of those whom he served, and ultimately, master of the destinies of Europe. It was Richelieu. In 1622 he was made Cardinal, and in 1624 he became Prime Minister of France, and soon subdued the nobility, and made the feeble Louis the most absolute monarch in Europe. *White's France. Richelieu in Am. Cy. Louis XIII. in Am. Cy.*

The Huguenots, determined to throw off the yoke which was
1628. made too oppressive, resorted to arms, and finally assembled at Rochelle with the purpose of establishing a republic. England attempted to aid the struggling Protestants, but the vigorous hand of Richelieu at last triumphed, and Rochelle, the last stronghold of the Huguenots, fell, after a siege of nearly a year.—*Modern Europe, Vol.* 1, *p.* 521. *White's France, p.* 315.

On the 4th of December, 1642, Richelieu died, and five
1643. months later, Louis XIII. followed his great minister to the grave. Louis XIV., not yet five years old, succeeded to a kingdom which the iron rule of a remorseless Cardinal had pressed into quiet. But even such quiet had produced physical prosperity and growth, though vice and folly abounded as always among an enslaved people. England was rocking in the waves of a terrible civil strife, but France lay bound, or rather tamed, to entire submission.

Another Cardinal, Mazarin, a disciple of Richelieu, succeeded as Prime Minister, and ruled in the same spirit. The queen-mother, Anne of Austria, daughter of Philip III. of Spain, was made Regent.—*Louis XIV. and Mazarin in Am. Cy.*

Richelieu, who hated the House of Hapsburg, had been a chief supporter of the Protestant arms in the Thirty Years' War, and in the last period of the war the French troops bore a great share of the burdens. In the battle of Rocroy the famous French general, the Great Conde, won a splendid victory over the Spaniards and Walloons who espoused the Austrian side.—*Modern Europe, Vol.* 1, *p.* 543.

France was one of the chief parties to the Peace of Westphalia

1648. which closed the Thirty Years' War. The French obtained, by this treaty, Alsace and some other places in Germany and Italy. The spirit of liberty, though crushed, was not dead in France.

The taxes having been greatly increased, a sullen resistance was roused. The opponents of Mazarin were called "Frondeurs," or Slingers, in derision of their flippant flings at the prime minister. The court party were called "Mazarins." At length Mazarin having resorted to violence, and proceeded to arrest some of the leaders, Paris rose in revolt.—*White's France, pp.* 331–335. *Fronde in Am. Cy.*

The Frondeurs of the Parliament of Paris compelled the court
1649. to retire to St. Germain, and Paris being now in the
hands of the insurgents, the Great Conde, with 7000 men, undertook to besiege it. But while the more earnest English republicans were gravely punishing their tyrant with death, these fickle Frondeurs made peace with theirs. The Fronde continued, but it was a series of intrigues without dignity or use; a mixture of masquerades and fights.—*White's France, p.* 336.

Mazarin, again resorting to violence, was compelled to flee
1651. from France, and took refuge at Cologne. But though
in exile, he continued to rule from his place of retreat.—*Mazarin in Am. Cy.*

The Fronde at length was suppressed, and Mazarin returned
1653. in triumph to France, the same year that Cromwell be-
came Lord Protector in England.—*White's France, pp.* 342, 343. *The Fronde in Am. Cy.*

Spain had assisted the Fronde, and France thus brought on
1655. a war in which England united. The Great Conde was
now fighting on the side of his former Spanish foes.—*White's France, pp.* 343, 344, *Mod. Europe, Vol.* 2, *pp.* 141, 142.

It was about this period that the haughty young king, when appealed to for some reform in the State, made the celebrated and significant reply, "I am the State." This was the culmination of absolutism. The people were nothing; the monarch was all.—*Louis XIV. in Am. Cy.*

The peace of Pyrenees, which closed the war between France

and Spain, restored the Conde to France, and confirmed
1659. the French possession of Alsace.—*Mod. Europe, Vol.* 2, *p.* 143.

Another result of the treaty of the Pyrenees was the marriage
of Louis with Maria Theresa, daughter of the Spanish
1660. king. In one of the marriage articles, the princess solemnly renounced all right she might ever have to the Spanish crown. And yet it was with an eye to this crown that the marriage was planned by Mazarin, and from this marriage sprang, finally, the Spanish Bourbons.—*White's France, p.* 345.

The death of Mazarin, which occurred this year, relieved the
young king from the control which had become irksome.
1661. His pride and ambition now had full sway, and he entered upon that career which made the "Age of Louis, the Fourteenth" the most brilliant era in French history. Louis was as autocratic as Napoleon, and, like Napoleon, he had the tact or good fortune to surround hinself with ministers of the most splendid talent.

Colbert, who succeeded Mazarin, was a man of great integrity and wonderful capacity—a second Sully.—*White's France, p.* 346.

Louis bought Dunkirk of Charles II. of England for £400,000
sterling. He often assisted the needy and reckless
1662. Charles, and thus bribed him to be friendly or neutral when the English were in opposition.—*White's France, p.* 351.

Louis, thirsting for military glory, asserted his wife's claims to
the Spanish Netherlands, her father having died in 1665.
1667. His victorious armies invaded these provinces, and, in one campaign,overrun the country.—*White's France, pp.* 351, 352.

Louis' rapid conquest of Flanders and Franche Comte stirred
the jealousy of other powers, and the Triple Alliance of
1668. England, Holland, and Sweden was formed to resist his further aggressions.

This alliance compelled Louis to sign the peace of Aix la Chapelle, and sullenly give back Franche Comte to Spain.—*White's France, p.* 353.

It was during this period that Louis erected the magnificent palace of Versailles, begun in 1664 and opened as the royal residence in 1681. The cost is stated to have been near $200,-000,000. Louis made magnificence a study, and practiced grandeur as an art. When he walked through his halls in pomp, his courtiers burst forth in applause. The excessive refinement and stately etiquette of the French Court were the envy and admiration of Europe, and by mere force of manners, *Le Grand Monarque* oppressed his fellow sovereigns, and ruled by his majestic deportment almost as much as by his arms.—*Louis XIV. and Versailles in Am. Cy. White's France.*

1672. Louis, enraged at the part Holland had taken in the Triple Alliance, bribed Charles of England not to interfere, and sent out his great generals, Conde and Turenne, who, in forty days, overrun the country. William of Orange, the great foeman of Louis, ordered the dykes to be cut and the ocean to be let in to stay the progress of the French.—*White's France, pp.* 356, 357.

1674. The English people compelled Charles to make peace with Holland and desert Louis. Several of the German States and Spain took sides with the Dutch. But the French continued victorious; and Turenne conquered at Sinsheim and Mulhausen.—*Mod. Europe, Vol.* 2, *pp.* 211, 212.

1675. Marshal Turenne was struck in the breast, with a bullet, as he was inspecting the enemy's work at Sasbach, and thus fell one of Louis' greatest generals.—*White's France, p.* 358.

1676. In three naval engagements in the Mediterranean, in one of which the great De Ruyter fell, the French fleets gained victories, and rode, for the time, masters of the Mediterranean.—*Mod. Europe, Vol.* 2, *p.* 214.

1677. The French gained another great victory over the Dutch at Mont Cassel. William of Orange was obliged to retire, and St. Omer fell into the hands of the French.—*White's France, p.* 360.

1678. The peace of Nimeguen closed the war of France with Holland and the other powers, the French retaining Franche Comte, now a part of France, and many large fortresses and towns in Flanders or Belgium.—*White's France, p.* 361.

Louis, having largely recruited his armies and fleets, seized
1681. Strasburg in the time of profound peace.—*White's France, p.* 364.

Genoa having given Louis offence, he sent a fleet which severely bombarded the town, destroying some of its finest streets and palaces. Thus he ruled Europe as with a rod of iron.—*Mod. Europe, Vol.* 2, *p.* 238.

Louis now proceeded to a stretch of power which was as fatal
1685. as it was foolish and wicked. He revoked the Edict of Nantes. The Huguenots, thus exposed to persecution, sadly deserted the land their industry had enriched, and carried their arts to England, Holland, Germany, and Sweden. The wise Colbert had died, 1683, and Louis was under the influence of Madame Maintenon, whom he had privately married.—*White's France, p.* 367. *Mod. Europe, Vol.* 2, *p.* 239.

The insolent aggressions of Louis again aroused the other
1686. powers, and the League of Augsburg was formed by Germany, Holland, and several other States. An army of 50,000 men was raised, and Louis, withdrawing in alarm from the Palatinate, ordered the country to be devastated to prevent the allies from following him.—*Abbott's Empire of Austria, p.* 315.

Louis' war with the League, at length begun, soon involved
1688. almost all Europe. In 1689, England, now under William III., joined the League.—*Abbott's Austria, p.* 316. *Modern Europe, Vol.* 2, *p.* 271.

At the great naval battle of La Hogue, already described
1692. under English events, Louis' naval power received a fatal blow. *White's France, p.* 371.

The French victories at Steinkirk, 1692, and at Neerwinden, 1693, have already been mentioned

The recapture of Namur by William, told that the tide of
1695. French affairs had turned. The great monarch at length began to yield.

Louis had lost his greatest ministers and generals, his people
696. were exhausted, and he began to long for peace.—*White's France, p.* 374.

The peace of Ryswick at length gave rest to weary and war-

1697. worn Europe. It gave back all the Flemish and other conquests of France, and compelled Louis to acknowledge his old foe, William of Orange, as king of England.—*White's France, p.* 374.

The accession of his grandson, Philip of Anjou, to the vacant throne of Spain, plunged Louis into the last and greatest
1700. of his wars.

SPAIN AND PORTUGAL.

THE tedious and dreary bigotry of Philip II. did its work; and when, at the close of the sixteenth century, the scepter fell into the hands of his indolent and imbecile son, Philip III., the united kingdoms of Spain and Portugal were like nations stricken with a palsy. Spain was no longer the great monarchy of Ferdinand and Isabella, and of their mighty grandson, Charles V. Its world-wide possessions were crumbling away from it, and its decadence hastened with accelerated pace.

Philip II. had married his daughter to Albert of Austria,
1604. and given her the Netherlands as a marriage portion. But the seven united provinces refused to submit to the new master, and both parties prepared for a more vigorous battle. Ostend, after a siege of three years, fell before the united forces of Austria and Spain.—*Mod. Europe, Vol.* 1. *p.* 500.

Spain, at length, wearied and hopeless, agreed to a truce of
1609. twelve years, and the Holland Republic was finally independent, while the ten provinces of the Spanish Netherlands remained under the Spanish yoke.—*Modern Europe, Vol.* 1, *p.* 502. *Netherlands in Am. Cy.*

This same year, the Spanish Monarch, in his folly, proceeded to drive out the remaining Moriscoes. This measure cost Spain nearly a million of its people.

Philip IV., who now succeeded his father, Philip III., was a

man of some talent and enterprize, but was largely
1621. under the influence of his ambitious minister, Olivarez, who sought to make Spain play its old part of power in the affairs of Europe, but only hastened its decay.—*Olivarez in Am. Cy. Modern Europe, Vol.* 1, *p.* 517.

The oppressive measures of Olivarez roused revolts in several of the Spanish provinces; and the Portuguese, taking
1640. advantage of the times, recovered their independence, and proclaimed the Duke of Braganza, king, under the title of John IV.—*Modern Europe, Vol.* 1, *p.* 538.

France, resenting the support Spain had given to the Fronde, declared war, and England joined in the struggle,
1655. tempted perhaps by the rich possessions which still remained to the Spaniards in America.—*Modern Europe, Vol.* 2, *p.* 141

The loss of Jamaica, 1655, the destruction of the Plate Fleet, 1656, and the close of the war by the Peace of the Pyrenees, have already been related under England and France.

On the death of Philip IV., he was succeeded by his son, Charles II., a feeble-minded, sickly boy, the last king of
1665. the House of Austria, or Hapsburg, in Spain.—*Modern Europe, Vol.* 2. *p.* 195.

The French king had married an elder sister of Charles, the daughter of Philip IV., by a former wife, and now
1667. claimed the Spanish Netherlands as her inheritance. The war with which he sought to enforce this claim, as also the peace of Aix la Chapelle, which closed the war, were given among French events.—*Modern Europe, Vol.* 2, *pp.* 195–197.

Charles II., after a long but imbecile and unfortunate reign, died without heirs, leaving poor Spain to become the
1700. tempting prize of the stronger powers. Louis XIV. had persuaded the feeble Charles to will the monarchy to his grandson, Philip of Anjou, who took possession of the throne, November 14, as Philip V. He was the first of the Spanish Bourbons. —*Abbott's Austria, pp.* 330, 331.

GERMANY.

At the opening of the seventeenth century, the throne of the German Empire was occupied by the imbecile Rudolph II., who preferred the study of astrology to the cares of sovereignty, and under whose neglect there were slowly gathering those elements of strife which were soon to break out in one of the longest and bloodiest wars of modern history. The German Empire had already declined largely from its former power, and its decadence was hastened by the Thirty Years' War. At the close of this century it began to brake into fragments, and after maintaining a powerless form for a hundred years longer, it finally disappeared from the family of nations.

The long truce between the different religious parties in the
1608. Empire began to be disturbed by the apprehensions that the probable successor of Rudolph was a bigoted Catholic. The Protestant princes accordingly formed the Protestant, or Evangelical Union for mutual defence.—*Kohlrausch's Germany, p.* 309.

The Duke of Cleves and Berg dying without heirs, a dispute
1609. arose about the succession. The emperor took one side; the Protestant Union the other; and Henry IV. of France prepared to put himself at the head of the Protestant party. He was assassinated in 1610, just as he was about to take the field. The Catholic princes formed, in opposition to the Union, the Catholic League, with Maximilian of Bavaria at its head. The dispute was amicably adjusted, but the rancor between the parties remained.—*Kohlrausch, p.* 310.

On the death of Rudolph, he was succeeded by his brother
1612. Matthias, who had already robbed the unhappy emperor of all his crowns except that of the empire. Matthias was an earnest Catholic, and his accession increased the gathering discontent. His choice of a still more bigoted Catholic, his

cousin Ferdinand, to succeed him, excited the most gloomy forebodings of the Protestants.—*Kohlrausch, pp.* 311–313.

The long smothered flame at length burst forth in the THIRTY YEARS' WAR. This war was nothing at first but a riotous
1618. insurrection in Bohemia, headed by Count Thurn, and consequent on the destruction of a Protestant church by order of the Catholic bishop. The emperor, having been appealed to, refused to grant redress. Two imperial councillors were thrown from a window in Prague, and the Protestants rushed to arms. —*Kohlrausch, p.* 314.

Matthias died March 10th, and was succeeded by his cousin, Ferdinand II., who had been educated as a Jesuit, and
1619. was an uncompromising hater of Protestantism. The Bohemians, a majority of whom were Protestants, deposed Ferdinand as king, and elected Frederick V. of the Palatinate, a son-in-law of James I. of England.—*Kohlrausch, pp.* 317, 318.

The imperial army met the Bohemians on the White Hill near Prague, and in less than an hour the fate of
1620. Bohemia was decided. Frederick fled from his capital, and Prague fell into the hands of Ferdinand.—*Kohlrausch, p.* 319.

After waiting about three months as if studying how most terribly to punish the rebels, Ferdinand suddenly ar-
1621. rested the Protestant leaders, and twenty-seven of them were tried and put to death. The Protestant religion was prohibited, and, after a series of persecutions, the Protestants were driven out, to the number of about 30,000 families, houseless and beggars, to become wanderers over Europe.—*Kohl., p.* 319.

After the capture of Prague, Count Mansfield, with some others, collected forces and kept up the war, till, finally,
1625. Christian IV. of Denmark was chosen to lead the Protestant forces. The war grew larger in its proportions. The several Protestant states, and England promised aid; and the Catholic forces were also increased.—*Kohlrausch, pp.* 320, 321.

After various operations, the Danish king met Tilly, the ablest general of the Catholic League, at Lutter, in Hanover,
1626. and was totally defeated with the loss of all his artillery. —*Kohlrausch, p.* 323.

Wallenstein, a great general of the emperor Ferdinand, and
1627. one of the most singular characters in that age, had raised 50,000 men at his own expense, and taken an active part in the war. He, now, in conjunction with Tilly, entered Holstein and overran Denmark, making fearful devastations.—*Kohlrausch, pp.* 322, 323. *Wallenstein in Am. Cy.*

Wallenstein, whose army was now increased to 100,000 men,
1628. and who had become the terror of all Germany, laid siege to Stralsund. After losing 12,000 men in useless assaults, he was compelled to abandon the siege.—*Kohlrausch, p.* 324.

Christian IV. abandoned the Protestant League, and made
1629. peace with the emperor at Lubec, the 12th of May. This closed the second or Danish period of the war. Protestant Germany seemed now to lie helpless at the feet of the merciless Ferdinand and his terrible general, and woes unutterable were visited upon the distracted country.—*Kohl. pp.* 324–326.

That great Christian hero, Gustavus Adolphus, king of
1630. Sweden, instigated and assisted by Richelieu, now espoused the cause of the Protestants, and landed in Germany with 15,000 men. Through the intrigues of Richelieu, Wallenstein was dismissed from his command and disbanded his army.—*Kohlrausch, p.* 327. *Richelieu in Am. Cy.*

While Gustavus was pursuing his victorious career, Tilly laid
1631. siege to Magdeburg. The Swedish king was hindered by the refusal of the timid Protestant princes to allow him passage, from reaching it in time for its relief. Its sack was one of the most terrible scenes in history.—*Kohl. pp.* 329–331.

On the 7th of September, Gustavus at length met Tilly at Breiteneld, near Leipsic, and fought with him his first great pitched battle. Tilly was utterly defeated, and the imperial army nearly destroyed. Gustavus marched in triumph to Mayence, on the Rhine, taking the principal cities on his route.—*Kohlrausch, p.* 332.

Gustavus next invading Bavaria, whose prince Maximilian was
1632. head of the Catholic League, met Tilly with a large army on the Lech, and again defeated him. Tilly re-

ceived in this battle a wound which resulted in his death a few days afterwards. This great general having fallen, Wallenstein was again recalled to the command. Raising a large army, he took the field. The armies met at Lutzen, the 16th of November, and victory declared for the Swedes; but their great king fell.—*Kohlrausch, pp.* 333–336.

Wallenstein carried on the war in so laggard a way that he
1634. was removed from command. It is asserted that he was in treaty with Richelieu to betray the emperor and join the Swedes. He was assassinated by the imperial soldiers. After his death, the chief command devolved on Ferdinand, the son of the emperor. He gained a great victory over the Swedes at Nordlingen, September 6th, and Germany seemed again prostrate at the feet of Ferdinand. But again the hand of Richelieu interfered, and French money soon equipped another powerful army. The war from this time was mostly a struggle of ambition and for empire.—*Kohlrausch, pp.* 340–342.

Ferdinand II. died, February 15th, without living to see the
1637. end of that terrible storm which his bigotry had aroused. He was succeeded by his son, Ferdinand III.—*Kohlrausch, p.* 342.

The war was continued under the great Swedish generals
1643. Bernard, of Weimar, Banner and Torstenson, who commanded in succession. The French generals, Conde and Turenne, also came into the field, and in the great battles of Freiburg and Nordlingen, they defeated the Spaniards, who had embraced the imperial cause.—*Kohlrausch, p.* 343. *White's France, pp.* 329, 330.

After four years of negotiations, the Peace of Westphalia was
1648. concluded, and the terrible Thirty Years' War ceased. This peace marked a great era in history, and readjusted the map of Europe.—*Kohlrausch, pp.* 343–348. *Mod. Europe, Vol.* 1, *p.* 550.

On the death of Ferdinand III., his son, Leopold I., was
1657. elected emperor, though the French monarch was a candidate for the imperial throne. Leopold's reign was chiefly occupied with wars against Louis XIV.—*Kohl., p.* 352.

The Turks continued to invade and harass Hungary and
other parts of the empire ; and, in this year, they passed
1683. through Hungary with 200,000 men, and laid siege to
Vienna itself. The emperor fled, but the brave Sobieski of Poland came to the aid of the Austrians, and, with Charles of Lorraine, attacked and repulsed the Turks, who fled, leaving an immense booty behind them.—*Kohlrausch, p.* 358.

Germany was a party to the League of Augsburg, formed
against Louis XIV., who had come to be considered as
1686. the common enemy of all Christendom.

The Turks were again totally defeated at Mohacz by Charles
of Lorraine, and, as a consequence, all Hungary sub-
1687. mitted to the House of Austria.—*Kohlrausch, p.* 360.

The war of the League of Augsburg with France having at
length begun, Germany was made the battle ground, and
1688. suffered many devastations.—*Kohlrausch, p.* 361.

Belgrade, which had been taken by the Turks in 1522, was this year retaken by the Austrians.—*Belgrade in Am. Cy.*

Germany was one of the parties to the Peace of Ryswick, and
received back only Strasburg, Brisach, and Philipsburgh,
1697. of the places conquered by the French.—*Kohl., p.* 362.

The emperor Leopold had married the second daughter of Philip IV. of Spain, and when, in 1700, the Spanish throne was left vacant, he asserted the right of his son Charles, Archduke of Austria, to succeed. Out of the conflicting claims of Charles and Philip of Anjou grew the war of the Spanish succession.—*Kohlrausch, p.* 363.

HOLLAND AND NETHERLANDS.

Holland, or the United Provinces, was still in the midst of its great struggle for independence when the seventeenth century opened. Ten of the provinces, those lying next to France, remained under the Spanish rule, and were known as the Spanish Netherlands. Philip II. had married his daughter to Albert of

Austria, and given her the Netherlands as a marriage portion. Spain, however, continued to support the war against the revolted provinces. The Hollanders, or Dutch, as they are called, were under the lead of Maurice, son of William of Orange, who proved himself one of the greatest generals of his age. Holland, during this century, rapidly rose to the rank of a leading power, and was, for a time, mistress of the seas.

After a siege of more than three years, the Spaniards succeeded
1604. in taking Ostend, but with the loss of nearly 80,000 men. While the Spanish forces were employed around Ostend, Maurice made conquests which more than compensated for its loss, and the Dutch extended their dominions in the East Indies and in America.—*Russell's Modern Europe, Vol.* 1, *p.* 501.

Spain, wearied with the long contest, at length agreed to the
1609. truce of the Hague for twelve years, leaving Holland, in the meantime, in possession of all her conquests. Holland, during this truce, was much rent with religious and civil dissentions, and Maurice was charged with attempts to usurp kingly power, and destroy the liberty of his country. The Dutch, however, continued their conquests abroad, settling, among other places, New York, in 1614.

On the accession of Philip IV. in Spain, the war was re-
1621. opened, and the Dutch, under Maurice, and, after his death in 1625, under his brother Henry, gained great advantages, conquering a large portion of Brazil, and greatly extending the Dutch empire in the East Indies. The war was finally closed by the peace of Westphalia.—*Netherlands in American Cy.*

Holland became engaged in a naval war with England. The
1652. events and fortunes of this war have already been noticed under England. It was terminated, in 1654, by the peace of Westminster.

Another war with England followed; the merchants of the two
1664. nations being engaged in a great rivalry for the trade of the world. The peace of Breda, concluded in 1667, closed this war. See England.

The statesmen of Holland now became the leading opponents

1668. of Louis XIV., whose conquests evidently looked to the annexation of the Netherlands to the French monarchy. The triple alliance of Holland, England, and Sweden forced the French king to let go his hold, for the time, of the Dutch provinces.

William III. of Orange was the son of William II., and of Mary,
1672. sister of Charles II. of England. His father had attempted to establish a despotism in Holland, and the House of Orange was in great disfavor. But in this year he was made Captain General. Holland had been attacked and overrun by Conde and Turenne, Louis' great generals. But William ordered the dykes to be cut, and so far restored the Dutch affairs, that Louis and Charles offered to make him absolute. But he declined their offer, and remained true to his country, and the unyielding foe of France. He was the greatest diplomatist of the age, and a great military leader. Though frequently defeated in battle, he rallied after each defeat with a fresh power. His various battles of Sinsheim, Mulhausen, in 1674, and of Mont Cassel, in 1677, are noticed under England and France.—*William III. of England in Am. Cy.*

William married his cousin Mary, daughter of James, Duke of
1677. York. This greatly increased his popularity with the English people, who looked upon him almost as one of their own princes.

William of Orange, who had come to be regarded as the
1688. champion of the popular party in England, invaded England with nearly 15,000 men, landing at Torbay, the 5th of November, and marching in triumph to London.—*Macaulay, Vol. 2, pp.* 375.

William and his wife Mary, were, after some delay and con-
1689. siderable debate, proclaimed joint sovereigns of England. William still remained Stadtholder of Holland, but the two countries continued distinct and independent.—*Macaulay, Vol. 2, p.* 512,

The great naval battle of La Hogue, already described under England, gave William a firmer seat on his throne, and greatly strengthened his power against France.

William commanded in person at the battle of Steinkirk, and suffered a severe defeat, but with unabated courage he still pressed on the war.

At Neerwinden, William was defeated again by the French general Luxemburg, with the loss of 14,000 men. The
1693. French did not follow up their victory, except to overrun and plunder Heidelberg, and some other German towns.—*Modern Europe, Vol.* 2. *p.* 277.

The siege and capture of Namur raised again the reputation of William, and helped the cause of the League.—*Mod-*
1695. *ern Europe, Vol.* 2, *p* 279.

The peace of Ryswick closed the war of the League. It restored the Spanish Netherlands to Spain, and acknow-
1697. ledged William's right to the throne of England.—*Modern Europe, Vol.* 2, *p.* 280.

NORTHERN AND EASTERN EUROPE.

The Northern and Eastern nations, Sweden, Denmark, Russia, Poland, and Turkey, at the opening of this century, held no prominent place in European affairs, except, perhaps, the Turks, who were the scourge and dread of the German Empire. During the century, Sweden, and afterwards Russia, came forward into the field of history, and became leading powers.

Gustavus Adolphus succeeded his father Charles IX. He was only 21 years old at his accession, and proved to be
1611. one of the greatest men of his age. Most of his life was spent in wars in Poland, Russia, and Germany, the affairs of his government being administered by the wise councillor Oxenstiern. The career of Gustavus in the Thirty Years' War has been noticed under Germany. After his death, the Swedes still participated in the war till its close, and gained some territory by the peace of Westphalia.—*Sweden in Am. Cy.*

Gustavus was succeeded on the throne by his little daughter

Christina, only six years of age; but the real ruler of Sweden was the wise Oxenstiern.

Christina, whose love of pleasure and of art made her averse to the cares of empire, abdicated her throne in favor of
1654. her cousin Charles X. After some brilliant but useless wars against Denmark, he died, 1660.—*Sweden in Am. Cy.*

Charles XI., son of Charles X. succeeded his father, and ruled thirty-seven years. His reign increased the power of
1660. Sweden, and left it firmly established for his great son.

Sweden, then the leading power in the north, took part in the Triple Alliance against Louis XIV. of France. See Eng-
1668. land.

The great Polish chieftain, John Sobieski, was elected by the diet of the Polish nobility, king of Poland. This ancient,
1674. and once extensive and powerful kingdom, was already in its decline. The neighboring states had already begun to prey upon and partition its territories, and the Turks frequently threatened to destroy it. Sobieski had the previous year routed the Turks, and soon after his election he resumed the war.—*Poland and John III. Sobieski in Am. Cy. Lamartine's Turkey, Vol.* 3, *p.* 397.

The Turks, with an immense army, laid siege to Vienna. Sobieski was persuaded by the ambassadors of the emperor
1683. and the Pope, to hasten to the rescue, and, in a short but terrible struggle, he defeated the Turks, and drove them through Hungary; thus saving by his valor one of those rapacious powers which were already seeking to swallow up his country. On his death, in 1696, Augustus, Elector of Saxony, was elected king of Poland.—*Poland in Am. Cy. Lamartine's Turkey, Vol.* 3, *pp.* 401–405.

The battle of Mohacz was fought, August 12th. The Turks suffered a decisive defeat. The first battle of Mohacz,
1687. in 1526, marked the beginning, and this last the end, of the Turkish sway in Hungary.—*Mohacz in Am. Cy.*

Belgrade, an important town and fortress lying on the frontiers of Turkey, was this year taken by the Austrian forces.
1688. Two years later it was retaken by the Turks. The

Turkish empire in Europe was now in a hopeless decline. Turkey has since been "the sick man" among nations.—*Lamartine's Turkey, Vol.* 3.

Peter I., the Great, was crowned with his half brother Ivan, as successor to his brother Fedor, in 1682, but it was not
1689. till 1689 that he escaped from the regency of his sister Sophia, and became the reigning Czar. Russia was, till this time, a barbarous country, and little known to Western Europe. It was frequently conquered and overrun by the Poles, even in the first half of this century. But Peter, a man of remarkable genius, and indomitable will, by dint of his own personal character and efforts, imported civilization, settled the government, and led Russia into the front rank of great powers.—*Peter I. in Am. Cy.*

Charles XII. succeeded to the throne of Sweden, on the death of his father, Charles XI. He was 15 years of age at the
1697. time of his accession, and gave but little promise of the wonderful military genius which afterwards made him one of the great captains of his age.—*Charles XII. in Am. Cy.*

Russia, Poland, and Denmark, encouraged by the youth and the fancied imbecility of Charles XII., formed an alliance
1699. to grasp such parts of the extensive territories of Sweden as they believed to belong to themselves.—*Charles XII. in Am. Cy.*

The Peace of Carlowitz, concluded between Austria, Poland, Russia, Venice, and Turkey, for twenty-five years gave Transylvania and Hungary to Austria, Azof to Russia, the Ukraine to Poland, with other possessions to the other powers. Austria, the hereditary domain of the House of Hapsburg, now became one of the largest realms in Europe.—*Modern Europe, Vol.* 2, *p.* 280.

The young king of Sweden met the hostilities against him with an energy that surprised all. Invading Denmark, and
1700. laying siege to Copenhagen, he compelled the Danes to sue for peace. Without waiting for reinforcements, he proceeded by forced marches, and, with 9,000 men, attacked and routed 40,000 Russians, who were besieging Narva.—*Charles XII. in Am. Cy.*

GENERAL VIEW

OF THE

EIGHTEENTH CENTURY.

No one word can fitly characterize the EIGHTEENTH CENTURY. It was a period of the wildest activity, and of mighty and incessant changes. Movements of the grandest character and of the widest influence were in constant progress. It was the era of politics. The increased power and prominence of the people in national affairs gave to political science and art a new importance, and great politicians abounded. But the greatest actors of the century were not men, but peoples.

And still grander than the peoples, were the popular ideas that now appeared in definite form, and wrought with resistless force. The rights and responsibilities of man as man; the natural equality and fraternity of men; the right of a people to a voice in their own government; the responsibility of rulers to those whom they govern; the divine origin, rights, and destiny of human society; the progressive character of human history; the real worth and grandeur of the human soul; the sacred freedom of conscience; and the freedom of thought and speech; these were the mighty ideas which evolved and moulded the history of this great century. They heaved with earthquake power the very foundations of human society.

The century was rendered remarkable by the appearance of new nations within the field of history. Russia came into view, just at the opening of the century, in deadly grapple with Sweden. Prussia appeared, for the first time, as a distinct kingdom. America, in the west, rose to her separate place in the family of nations, and, in the east, the great empire of the British East Indies appeared. The old German Empire gradually falling to pieces, the Austrian Empire was seen in its place, sharing with

Prussia its territories, except such as rose to the rank of independent states or kingdoms.

Another, though less important feature of this period, were the wars of succession—the struggles for vacant thrones—four of which occurred within the century.

But the grand events which marked this era of history for all time, and gave it a place never to be forgotten, were the American and the French revolutions—the mighty struggle of oppressed but enlightened peoples for the broadest principles of personal and popular liberty. The great lessons of the century center in these two revolutions. America, rebellious against ancient falsehood and tyranny, but loyal to ancient faiths, rose to a regulated and permanent liberty. France, revolting alike against royalty and religion, against the Bourbons and the Bible, staggered blindly into the embrace of a despotism more terrible than that which she had overthrown.

The printing press had made literature a power; and the enfranchisement of thought and belief stimulated the growth of literature to the highest degree. Great writers abounded, and started revolutions with their pens, which monarchs could not stop with their swords.

The literature of the Eighteenth Century was of unsurpassed brilliance. It was the age of Pope, Johnson, Goldsmith, Cowper, Campbell, Burns, and Young; of Hume, Gibbon, and Robertson; of Voltaire, Rosseau, Rollin, Diderot, and D'Alembert; of Klopstock, Wieland, Lessing, Herder, Goethe, and Schiller.

In science appear the great names of Sir Isaac Newton, William Herschel, Linnæus, Count Buffon, and Franklin.

Hosts of writers and scholars are scattered through the century like points of light, making it gleam like a mental milky-way.

AMERICA

THE American colonies were rapidly growing into power and importance at the opening of the Eighteenth Century; but they were all, still, dependent colonies. In all the length and breadth of the continent, there was not one independent state. South and Central America were held chiefly by the Spanish and Portuguese, while the region north of the Gulf of Mexico belonged almost exclusively to France and England. These two nations were struggling for the lion's share of this best part of the new world, and their colonies were plunged into frequent wars to forward the designs of the mother countries. But these struggles taught the colonies their strength, and compelled them to that union of effort so necessary to their independence. It was impossible that American independence should be longer delayed; neither the ideas nor circumstances of Americans would permit it.

In June, Cadillac, with a Jesuit missionary and 100 Frenchmen, took possession of Detroit, and commenced a per-
1701. manent settlement. This was part of the French plan to
keep the great lakes for themselves.—*Bancroft, Vol.* 3, *p.* 194.

Queen Anne's War in America was contemporary with the war
of the Spanish succession in Europe. It was, indeed,
1702. only the American side of this war. It was opened by
Gov. Moore, of South Carolina, who led a force to attack St. Augustine, the Spanish capital of Florida. The town was ravaged, but two Spanish ships appearing, Moore retreated.—*Bancroft, Vol.* 3, *p.* 209.

In the north, the French and Indians burst upon New England,
prowling around all the northern and newer settlements.
1704. On the 1st of March, a war party attacked Deerfield, and
killed or made captive most of its citizens.—*Bancroft, Vol.* 3, *p.* 213.

In revenge for Gov. Moore's invasion of Florida, the French
and Spaniards attacked Charleston; but the invaders
1706. were bravely repulsed, with severe loss.—*Bancroft, Vol.*
3, *p.* 211.

The savage war went on in the north till the outrages of the
French roused in New England the greatest hatred
1710. against them. After repeated attempts, a strong fleet
was fitted out, and Acadia and Port Royal fell into the hands of the English and colonists. Acadia was annexed to the English

colonies as Nova Scotia. Thus the English extended their boundaries north and south.—*Bancroft, Vol.* 3, *p.* 218.

Another fleet, fitted out for the conquest of Canada, and placed under the command of Sir H. Walker, ran
1711. blindly on the rocks at the mouth of the St. Lawrence. Walker lost eight ships and nearly a thousand men, and returned discouraged to England.—*Bancroft, Vol.* 3, *pp.* 220–224. *Lossing, p.* 136.

The Fox Indians planned the destruction of Detroit, but friendly tribes rallying to the aid of the few French
1712. soldiers, this important place was saved to the French.—*Bancroft, Vol.* 3, *p.* 224.

The Peace of Utrecht, which closed the war of the Spanish succession, ended also Queen Anne's War. It confirmed
1713, Nova Scotia and the Hudson Bay region to England, but still left Louisiana to France.—*Bancroft, Vol.* 3, *p.* 233.

Law's gigantic Stock Company for settling and trading with the Mississippi regions, stimulated emigration, and a
1718. party founded a colony at New Orleans.—*Bancroft, Vol.* 3, *p.* 351.

The government of Massachusetts established Fort Dummer on the site of Brattleboro, and thus began the settlement
1724. of Vermont.—*Bancroft, Vol.* 3, *p.* 370.

Vitus Behring, a Swedish explorer, discovered the northeastern headland of Asia, and the straits which separate the old
1728. world from the new.—*Behring's Island in Am. Cy.*

The same year, or in 1730, according to some, the diamond mines of Golconda, in Brazil, were discovered.—*Diamonds in Am. Cy.*

After some trouble with the colonists, the proprietors of the Carolinas sold their rights to the English government,
1729. and the two provinces were separated and royal governors appointed over them.—*Bancroft, Vol.* 3, *p.* 331. *Lossing, p.* 171.

George Washington, the great American patriot, general, and statesman, was born, February 22d, in Westmoreland
1732. County, Virginia. The anniversaries of his birthday

are now observed as holidays.—*George Washington in Am. Cy.*

General Oglethorpe led a colony from England who settled at Savannah, and thus introduced Georgia, the last of
1733. the old Thirteen, into the circle of the English colonies. —*Lossing, p.* 100.

In 1739, England had become involved in a war with Spain, on account of the piracies of British vessels on the
1742. Spanish colonies. In 1741, an attack was made upon Carthagena, a strong Spanish town on the northern coast of South America. Attempts were also made to extend English rule over Florida. In June, 1742, a large Spanish fleet was sent to subdue Georgia, but the brave Oglethorpe successfully defended his little colony.—*Bancroft, Vol.* 3, *pp.* 440–446.

The war of the Austrian succession, which began in 1740, soon involved the other European powers, and, of
1744. course, their American colonies. In 1744, France and England came to open war. The American part of this war is known as King George's War.—*Ban., Vol.* 3, *p.* 457. *Los. p.* 136.

The principal event of King George's War was the capture, by American and English forces, of Louisburg, "the
1745. Gibraltar of America." The next year the French attempted in vain to recover the place.—*Lossing, pp.* 137, 138.

In the treaty of Aix la Chapelle, which closed the war, Louisburg was restored to the French, and the colonies
1748. gained nothing by their sacrifices, but the knowledge of their strength, and the habit of co-operation.—*Lossing, p.* 138. *Bancroft, Vol.* 3, *p.* 466.

June 15, Franklin, by means of a kite, succeeded in drawing electricity from a thunder cloud, and thus demon-
1752. strated the fact that the terrible lightning, so long the terror of mankind, is nothing but electricity. Some European naturalists, following out Franklin's suggestions, had made the same discovery in May, but the credit still rests with Franklin. —*Lightning in Am. Cy.*

The French had determined to confine the English colonies to the region east of the Alleghanies, and to exclude
1753. them entirely from the great valley of the Mississippi.

They stirred up the Indians against some English settlers on the Ohio, and both parties began to erect forts to secure the country. At length Governor Dinwiddie, of Virginia, sent out young Washington, as a special messenger, to gain information, and to carry a protest to the French Commandant. The commission was executed with success, though with much difficulty and danger.—*Bancroft*, *Vol.* 4, *pp.* 108–112.

The final struggle of the French and English for the possession of North America finally broke out in the conflict known
1754. in American history as the "*French and Indian War.*" Washington was sent out with a regiment of 150 men, to strengthen the fort erected at the place where Pittsburg now stands, but before he could reach it, the French had captured the fort, and changed its name to fort Du Quesne. Meeting the French, May 27th, at Great Meadows, Washington attacked and defeated them, killing their commander. Hearing that a larger force was advancing against him, he fell back to a rude stockade he had erected, and named Fort Necessity. This he defended with such bravery, that he was permitted to withdraw in honor.—*Bancroft*, *Vol.* 4, *pp.* 117–121.

In June, the Congress of Commissioners from the several colonies met at Albany, to consult for the general defence.—*Bancroft*, *Vol.* 4. *p.* 121.

Three expeditions were planned for this year against the French; one against Fort Du Quesne, another against
1755. Niagara and Frontenac, and the third against Crown Point. That against Du Quesne was led by General Braddock, who, refusing the counsel of Washington, who was acting as his aid, fell into an ambush about ten miles from the fort, and was defeated and slain, July 9th. The two other expeditions were also unsuccessful; but a fourth, fitted out by New England against Acadia, was successful. The victors, with an excess of severity, utterly destroyed the French settlements, and scattered the peaceful settlers.—*Los.*, *pp.* 185–189. *Ban.*, *Vol.* 4, *pp.* 184–193.

On the 17th of May, England formally declared war against France, and sent Lord Loudon, as Commander-in-Chief,
1756. with General Abercrombie as his lieutenant. The cam-

paign was an unfortunate one for the colonies. Oswego was taken by the French.—*Lossing, pp.* 191, 192. *Bancroft, Vol.* 4, *p.* 233, *and pp.* 236–243.

The English were still unfortunate. The tardy Loudon planned, and then relinquished, a campaign against
1757. Louisburg. Montcalm, with his French and Indians, captured Fort William Henry, on Lake George, and massacred the brave garrison, which had surrendered.—*Lossing, p.* 194. *Bancroft, Vol.* 4, *pp.* 262–266.

Pitt now ruled in England, and the tide of affairs turned. Generals Amherst and Wolfe attacked and conquered
1758. Louisburg.—*Bancroft, Vol,* 4, *pp.* 296,297. *Lossing,* 196.

The poor, incompetent, Abercrombie led a grand expedition against the French, at Ticonderoga, but was miserably repulsed, with heavy loss.—*Lossing, p.* 197.

General Forbes led another expedition against Fort Du Quesne. He finally, after much delay, sent Washington forward, who found the fort deserted. In the meantime, Ft. Frontenac fell into the hands of the Americans, and the French power in America was hopelessly crippled.—*Ban., Vol.* 4, *pp.* 308, 312, 313. *Los., p.* 198.

Pitt now planned the conquest of Canada, and the total annihilation of the French power in America. General Am-
1759. herst was sent out, and captured Ticonderoga and Crown Point, and drove the French from the region of Lake Champlain. Sir William Johnson, who succeeded General Prideaux, took Fort Niagara, and broke the great chain of French fortresses, which linked Canada and Louisiana. But the grand event of the year was the capture of Quebec by the heroic Wolfe, who fell in the hour of victory. The brave French General Montcalm also fell in the same battle. Montreal still remained to the French, but their power was hopelessly broken.—*Bancroft, Vol.* 4, *pp.* 319–338. *Lossing, pp.* 199–203.

The French made an ineffectual attempt to regain Quebec. But their hour had come, and, unable to resist the
1760. gathering forces of Amherst, they surrendered Montreal, and all their forts in Canada and Michigan; and French dominion in the north ceased forever.

The colonies had encountered great sacrifices ; but they had learned great and useful lessons. Parliament voted them about one million dollars, in addition to former grants, for their losses, but daily grew jealous of their increasing power.—*Bancroft, Vol.* 4, *pp.* 359–364. *Lossing, pp.* 203, 204, *and p.* 206, *note.*

In the south, the French still had Louisiana, and stimulated the Indians to ravage the frontiers of the Carolinas. The Indians were finally conquered, and compelled to sue for peace, June 1761.—*Lossing, p.* 204.

The first struggle between the Crown and the colonies occurred on the claim to the Writs of Assistance, com-
1761. manding colonial officers to enforce the acts of trade.
The fiery James Otis resisted successfully with his burning eloquence, and the Crown was defeated.—*Bancroft, Vol.* 4, *p.* 414.

England sent an expedition, composed partly of colonial forces,
against Havana, which, after a difficult siege, surrendered.
1762. *Bancroft, Vol.* 4, *pp.* 444, 445.

The Peace of Paris closed the war between England, France,
and Spain. It confirmed to England Canada, Acadia,
1763. and all of Louisiana east of the Mississippi.—*Bancroft,*
Vol. 4, *p.* 452.

In this same year the great chief Pontiac began a fierce Indian war against the western colonies.—*Lossing, p.* 205.

The war was ended, but another and grander struggle was already begun. England had triumphed over France in
1764. their contest for the sovereignty of North America. She
was now to grapple with her own colonies for the same great prize. The colonies were awake, and Pennsylvania, in October, sent Benjamin Franklin to England to represent her cause. He soon became the representative of American liberty.—*Bancroft, Vol.* 5, *p.* 220.

On the 27th of February, after long and violent debates on
both sides of the ocean, the House of Commons passed
1765. the famous Stamp Act, requiring revenue stamps to be
affixed to all legal papers, and on the 8th of March it passed the House of Lords. It was the assertion of the absolute power of Parliament over the American people, and was the first direct

blow struck in the American Revolution. The news was received in America with universal indignation. A Congress of delegates from several colonies met in New York, and it was soon evident that execution of the act would be resisted against the whole power of England.—*Bancroft, Vol.* 5, *pp.* 230–247, *and* 308. *Lossing, pp.* 213–215.

The firm protest of America against the Stamp Act, seconded
by the merchants of London, whose trade was being in-
1766. jured, led Parliament to consent to its repeal. This
repeal, effected in January, was received with bonfires, and universal rejoicings, both in England and America.—*Lossing, pp.* 216, 217. *Bancroft, Vol.* 5, *p.* 445.

In June, Parliament, in the absence of Pitt, who opposed such
measures, passed an act imposing duties upon tea, glass,
1767. paper, paints, &c., imported into the colonies. This
aroused anew the storm of excitement in America. Non-importation associations were founded, and the spirit of resistance gained new power.—*Los., p.* 218. *Ban., Vol.* 6, *pp.* 80, *and* 96.

Parliament grew obstinate and determined as American resistance to their acts increased, and, finally, Boston having
1768. prevented the collection of the Customs, a British force
of seven hundred men were sent, under General Gage, to overawe the citizens. These troops landed, October 1st, and encamped on the Common. It was a fatal blunder for England. The excitement in America became intense.—*Lossing, p.* 220. *Bancroft, Vol.* 6, *p.* 208. *Pictorial Eng., Vol.* 4, *p.* 869.

The troops in Boston were a source of constant irritation.
Quarrels frequently occurred, and, finally, on the 5th of
1770. March, a squad of eight soldiers fired on a crowd of
citizens, killing three, and wounding others. This was the famous "Boston Massacre." Here the first blood in the Revotion was shed.—*Bancroft, Vol.* 6, *pp.* 335–340.

The southern colonies were also bent on resisting. Associations, calling themselves *Regulators*, were formed in the
1771. Carolinas. Gov. Tryon marched a force against them,
and, after a bloody skirmish, dispersed them, capturing and hanging several leaders.—*Los., p.* 223. *Ban., Vol.* 6, *pp.* 390–397.

Parliament had, in 1770, taken off the tax from all articles except tea; but the Americans, now fully roused to
1773. opposition, refused to pay even this, and would not import, or use, the taxed luxury. At length the East India Company determined to send over, on their own account, some of the heavy surplus that had accumulated in their store houses. Cargoes were shipped to Charleston, Philadelphia, New York, and Boston. At New York and Philadelphia the landing was prevented. At Charleston, the tea was landed but not sold. At Boston, the Governor attempted to enforce the landing, but, December 16th, a party of citizens, disguised as Indians, went aboard the vessels, and threw the tea overboard. The "Boston Tea Party," as it was called, roused the wrath of Parliament, and helped to hasten the final collision.—*Lossing, p.* 224. *Bancroft, Vol.* 6, *pp.* 476–488.

To punish Boston for this act of defiance, Parliament enacted, March 7th, the Boston Port Bill, closing the port, and
1774. removing the public offices to Salem. Great distress followed in the martyr-city; but provisions and supplies were sent from all parts of the country.—*Lossing, pp* 225, 226.

The sufferings of Boston aroused the whole country: the storm of excitement became a whirlwind. A Congress was called, and on the 5th day of September, the FIRST CONTINENTAL CONGRESS met in Philadelphia.—*Lossing, p.* 228, *Bancroft, Vol.* 7, *p.* 127.

AMERICAN REVOLUTION.—On the 19th of April, the long pending struggle of arms began at the battle of Lexing-
1775. ton. Eight hundred British soldiers met seventy American minute men, and, firing upon them, killed eight, wounded several, and dispersed the remainder. It was a mere skirmish, but it opened the long and bloody drama of seven years of war. It kindled all the colonies into flame.—*Bancroft, Vol.* 7, *Chap.* 27. *Lossing, p.* 232.

In May, Crown Point and Ticonderoga were captured by some New England militia, with large quantities of cannon and military stores. On the 17th of June was fought the battle of Bunker Hill. The Americans were driven from their position, but their forces remained around Boston, and commenced a regular siege. *Bancroft, Vol.* 7, *p.* 339 *and Chap.* 39. *Lossing, pp.* 233–236.

Congress met May 10th, and, on the 15th of June, elected Washington Commander-in-Chief.

In the autumn of 1775, the Americans, under Arnold and Montgomery, invaded Canada, and attempted the capture of Quebec. The attack was unsuccessful, and by the middle of the next June, they were driven out of Canada, and that province thus failed to become a part of the United States.—*Lossing, pp.* 240–242.

On the 17th of March, Washington compelled the British to
1776. evacuate Boston. An American force marched at once to New York, anticipating an attack there.—*Bancroft, Vol.* 8, *pp.* 295–303.

A British fleet made an attack upon Fort Moultrie, Charleston, June 28th, but was repulsed with terrible havoc and loss.—*Lossing, pp.* 247–249. *Bancroft, Vol.* 8, *pp.* 401–410.

Declaration of Independence. On the Fourth of July, Congress deliberately declared the colonies independent of British rule, and decreed the separate national existence of the United States of America.—*Bancroft, Vol.* 8, *Chap.* 70.

The British, repulsed from Charleston, landed on Staten Island, where another British force was already assembled. On the 27th of August, was fought the battle of Long Island, in which the Americans were defeated by an overwhelming force of English and Hessians. This compelled Washington to evacuate New York.—*Lossing, pp.* 252–257. *Bancroft, Vol.* 9, *Chap.* 4.

The American affairs continued unfortunate, and the year was closing in the deepest gloom, when, on the 26th of December, Washington gained the brilliant victory of Trenton, and lightened the hearts and hopes of his countrymen—*Lossing, p.* 262. *Bancroft, Vol.* 9, *pp.* 231–235.

On the 3d of January, Washington, having escaped from before
1777. the British army sent against him, suddenly fell upon the enemy's reserve at Princeton, and gained another cheering victory. These victories saved American Independence. —*Lossing, pp.* 268, 269. *Bancroft, Vol.* 9, *pp.* 244–251.

At Brandywine and Germantown, Washington suffered some defeats, and was compelled to give up Philadelphia.—*Lossing, pp.* 272–275.

But victories were gained at Bennington (Lossing, p. 277.) and at Stillwater (Lossing, p. 281.), over Burgoyne, who was leading an English army from Canada by the way of Lake Champlain to cut the colonies in twain.

The victory over Burgoyne gave America foreign allies, and assured her independence. Young Lafayette did not, however, wait for our success, but came over at once, in a vessel fitted out at his own expense, and offered his services to America.—*Los.*, 273. *Bancroft, Vol.* 9, *Chap.* 16.

In February, while the American army was passing the terrible
1778. winter at Valley Forge, France recognised the independence of the United States, and formed a treaty with them, in accordance with which a French fleet was sent over to assist in the war. The English Parliament offered to repeal all obnoxious acts, and sent commissioners over to make peace ; but it was too late, Independence had been declared, and would not be relinquished.—*Lossing, pp.* 285, 286. *Bancroft, Vol.* 9, *Chap.* 29.

On the 28th of June was fought the terrible battle of Monmouth. The Americans slept on the field, but the British withdrew in the night.—*Lossing, p.* 288.

The frightful massacre at Wyoming occurred July 5th. The British again attacking the southern colonies, took Savannah, and made it their head quarters in the south.—*Los., pp.* 290–292.

The condition of affairs was gloomy. The country was overwhelmed with debt. The paper currency was nearly
1779. worthless. The French had failed to render any valuable assistance, and the heavy taxes disaffected many of the weaker patriots. Washington determined to act on the defensive.—*Lossing, pp.* 292–294.

The field of war was transferred by the English Commander, to the south. Many of the people of the south deserted the cause of freedom, and armed bands of tories roamed the country. At the battle of Brier Creek, March 3d, General Ashe, the

American Commander, was surprised and defeated, and his army nearly destroyed.—*Lossing, p.* 295.

At Stono Ferry, June 20th, the Americans attacked the British, but were repulsed. The heat then closed the campaign at the south. In the north, marauding parties were sent out by General Clinton, from New York, to ravage the towns in Connecticut and in Virginia, and an expedition up the Hudson captured, after a stout resistance, the fort at Stony Point. But six weeks later, General Wayne, by one of the bravest actions in the war, recaptured this fort, with a large amount of military stores, and a loss to the British of 600 men. By another daring exploit, Major Henry Lee captured the English garrison at Paulus Hook, or Jersey City.—*Lossing, pp.* 296–298.

In the west, the British from Detroit retook Vincennes, but Major Clark, penetrating the "drowned lands," with a force of 175 men, recaptured the place. General Sullivan pushing into the wilderness of southern New York, defeated the British and Indians at Chemung, now Elmira, and destroyed forty Indian villages.

In September, the Americans, aided by a French fleet, undertook the siege of Savannah. After severe losses, the siege was abandoned on account of the withdrawal of the French fleet just when the American Commander felt sure of victory.—*Los., p.* 305.

The prospect seemed dark and discouraging at the opening of
this year. The French alliance had produced no fruits,
1780. and the English Parliament seemed determined to put
forth their mightiest efforts.

The main body of the British force went south, and again undertook the siege of Charleston. After enduring the siege forty days, the city surrendered, May 12th, and General Lincoln and the American army became prisoners of war.—*Lossing, pp.* 309–311.

The Americans suffered another terrible defeat and loss on the Waxhaw.—*Lossing, p.* 313.

The south seemed entirely conquered, and Clinton, with the main army, returned to New York. The brave partisan leaders, Marion and Sumter, kept up hostilities, and Congress sent

General Gates to retrieve affairs, but he was severely beaten near Camden, and fled north, and shortly after, Sumter's force was nearly annihilated. Marion, with his brave but ragged and half starved followers, alone remained in arms in South Carolina to dispute the triumphant British power. His frequent and singular victories sustained the sinking courage of the country, and gave time for the patriots to rally.

In the north, the British attacked General Green, at Springfield, New Jersey, and were repulsed. Another French fleet came over, but too late to accomplish anything this year.—*Lossing, pp.* 320–323.

The darkest event of the year was the treason of Benedict Arnold, one of the bravest of the American generals, but extravagant and unprincipled, who now bargained to surrender the strong fortress of West Point to General Clinton. His treason was discovered and his designs prevented, but he escaped.—*Lossing, pp.* 324–326.

The seventh year of the war found England discouraged by the heavy loss and expenses of the conflict. Spain had

1781. declared against her, and Holland was known to be secretly negotiating with the United States. Still the ministry were obstinate, and large preparations were made to continue the war.

Arnold, now a British general, led an expedition up the James River, destroyed the public stores collected at Richmond, and devastated the country.

The war again raged in the south. General Green superseded Gates, and at the Cowpens, January 17th, the British were defeated by General Morgan, with heavy loss. General Cornwallis now commenced a pursuit of Green and Morgan, who wonderfully escaped into Virginia. Having recruited his forces, Green again advanced into North Carolina, and, March 15th, fought and lost the battle of Guilford Court House; but the British loss was also very severe. On the 25th of April, Green was again beaten; but not disheartened, he pushed the campaign with vigor, capturing post after post from the enemy. On the 8th of September, was fought the battle of Eutaw Springs, in which both parties claimed the victory. The English soon had nothing left them in South Carolina and Georgia, except Charleston and Savannah.—*Lossing, pp.* 330–338.

Cornwallis, after devastating Virginia, had retired to Yorktown. Here he was besieged by Washington and the French, and, on the 19th of October, surrendered with his whole army. —*Lossing, pp.* 338–341.

British statesmen felt that the defeat of Cornwallis had destroyed all hopes of the subjugation of America; and, in
1782. March, measures were introduced into Parliament for the cessation of hostilities. In America, the tories flocked back in thousands to the side of their country, and accepted the offered pardon. In July, the British evacuated Savannah. In August and September, skirmishes were fought with the British foraging parties sent out from Charleston, and with these the fighting ended. On the 14th of December, Charleston was evacuated, and the British withdrew from all posts but New York. A preliminary treaty of peace was signed at Paris, the 30th of November.—*Lossing, p.* 348.

The final, definitive treaty of Peace between England, France, and the United States was not signed till the 3d of Sep-
1783. tember. This has been called the Peace of Versailles. It embraced also Spain and Holland.—*Pict. Eng., Vol.* 5, *p.* 396. *Lossing, p.* 348.

Peace did not at once bring quiet and security. The country was deeply in debt. The currency was nearly worthless; industry and trade were prostrated. All minds looked gloomily into the uncertain future, and not a few wished Washington to assume the reigns of government as a king,

On the 25th of November, the British troops evacuated New York, and took their leave of American soil. In December, Washington bade an affectionate farewell to his officers and troops, and, a few days later, tendered to Congress his resignation. History can furnish no more illustrious instance of disinterested patriotism: ages will admire its grandeur.—*Irving's Life of Washington, Vol.* 4, *Chap.* 33. *Lossing, pp.* 351, 352.

In May, a Constitutional Convention met in Philadelphia, to

form a better and a stronger Union: Washington pre-
1787. sided. When no longer bound together by the common dangers of the war, it was found that the governments of the separate States were too strong, and the central government too weak for a time of peace. The labors of this august Convention, which closed in September, resulted in the formation of our present Constitution and Union.—*Los., pp.* 356–359. *Irving's Life of Washington, Vol.* 4, *Chap.* 36.

Shays' Rebellion was an insurrection in Massachusetts, under the lead of Daniel Shays, occasioned by the heavy burdens of the people, and by the attempt to raise, by direct taxation, the means to pay off the war debts.—*Los., p.* 353. *Shays in Am. Cy.*

Eleven States having ratified the new Constitution, Washington, on the 6th of April, was unanimously chosen the
1789. first President, and John Adams, Vice President. On the 30th of April, be was inaugurated in New York City.—*Lossing, pp.* 365, 366. *Irving's Washington, Vol.* 4, *Chap.* 37.

English agents from Canada continued to excite disturbances among the Indians, till finally the Indians began hos-
1790. tilities against the United States. General Harmer was sent against them, and was defeated in two battles near Fort Wayne, Indiana. The war continued till August, 1795.

Vermont, which had been claimed both by New York and New Hampshire, and had frequently demanded admis-
1791. sion into the confederacy, was now received as the fourteenth State in the American Union.—*Vermont in Am. Cy.*

General St. Clair, marching against the Indians in the Indian war then raging, was surprised and terribly defeated, losing 600 men.—*Lossing, p.* 374.

June 1st, Kentucky, the fifteenth State, was admitted into the Union.—*Kentucky in Am. Cy.*

1792. This year Washington was unanimously re-elected to the Presidency, and on the 4th of March, 1793, entered upon his second term.—*Irving's Washington, Vol.* 5, *Chap.* 17.

In June, Tennessee, which had originally been a part of North Carolina, was admitted into the family of States.—
1796. *Lossing, p.* 382. *Tennessee in Am. Cy.*

Differences of opinion in regard to the policy of the nation
were early developed, and these differences soon gave
1797. rise to two parties; the *Republicans*, who regarded Jefferson as their leader, and the *Federalists*, who counted Hamilton as their chief. Washington having declined to serve a third term, the Federalists nominated John Adams, and the Republicans, Thomas Jefferson, to succeed him. Adams was elected President, and Jefferson, having the next highest number of votes, became, by the Constitution, Vice President. They were inaugurated March 4th, 1797—*Lossing, p.* 382.

On the 14th of December, Washington died at Mount Vernon,
at the age of 68 years. The nation mourned his loss as
1799. that of a father.—*Irving's Washington, Vol.* 5, *Chap.* 34.

The close of the century found the United States sixteen in number, and rapidly increasing in population, prosperity, and power. The census of 1800 showed a population of 5,319,762 souls.

ENGLAND

The Eighteenth was an eventful Century in English history. Besides the brave part England played in European affairs, in this century, it won the French American colonies, and lost its own.

The sceptre of Great Britain rested, at the opening of the century, in the hands of that great and indomitable ruler, William III., Prince of Orange, the life-long foeman of the arrogant and ambitious Louis XIV., whose power, though in its decadence, still overshadowed Europe. England, under William, was great and powerful, and played a most important part among the States of Europe. At the opening of the century, William was supporting the young Charles XII. of Sweden against his rapacious neighbors, and was also engaging Europe to resist the accession of Louis' grandson, Philip V., to the throne of Spain. He saw that the union of the French and Spanish monarchies, in the hands of Louis, would be dangerous, and hence determined to support the claims of Charles of Austria to the Spanish succession. Internally, England was rent with the party strifes of the Whigs and Tories, the latter of whom had now obtained again the control of affairs.

Poor James II. died, September 16th, at the palace of St. Germain, where he had lived a dependent on the bounty
1701. of the French monarch. His son immediately assumed the title of James III., and was proclaimed as such by Louis. This helped to kindle the flame of war now ready to break out. In England he was known as "the Pretender."—*James II. in Am. Cy. Pict. Eng., Vol.* 4, *p.* 114.

On the 8th of March, William III. died, and was succeeded by Anne, daughter of James II., and wife of George,
1702. Prince of Denmark. With Anne, the Tories came into power, with the Duke of Marlborough at their head. The Duchess of Marlborough was a favorite of Anne, and exercised an almost complete control over her.—*Pict. Eng., Vol.* 4, *pp.* 123, *and* 125–127. *Anne in Queens of Eng., Vol.* 11, *p.* 866.

The War of the Spanish Succession, which began this year, involved nearly all Europe. The claims of Philip V., the French claimant for the Spanish throne, vacated by the death of Charles II. in 1700, were supported by France, with Bavaria, Cologne, and the western part of Spain. The claims of Charles, son of the emperor, Leopold I., were supported by England, Holland, Prussia, Germany, Savoy, Portugal, and a part of Spain. The Duke of Marlborough, and Eugene of Savoy, two of the greatest generals of the age, commanded the English and Allies.—*Mod. Europe, Vol.* 2, *pp.* 307–309. *Kohlrausch's Germany, p.* 366.

The war had been waged with varying success, but on the 13th of August, the great victory of Blenheim, or Hochstadt,
1704. was won by Marlborough and Eugene over the French and Bavarians. It was the most disastrous defeat yet inflicted on Louis, and was hailed throughout Europe with extravagant joy. The French lost nearly 40,000 men.—*Mod. Europe, Vol.* 2, *p.* 314. *Pict. Eng., Vol.* 4, *pp.* 155–158.

Gibraltar, which was deemed impregnable, was also taken by assault by the English sailors.—*Mod. Europe, Vol.* 2, *p.* 315.

Not much had been accomplished on either side in the year
1705, except some advantages gained over the French
1706. in Spain. On the 23d of May, Marlborough won
another splendid victory at Ramillies, the French losing 100
cannon and nearly 20,000 men. This victory gave to the allies
a large territory, and resulted also in heavy losses to the French
in Italy.—*Mod. Europe, Vol.* 2, *pp.* 319, 320.

On the 24th of April, the French gained a great victory over
the allies at Almanza. This victory established Philip
1707. V. firmly on the throne.—*Mod. Europe, Vol.* 2. *p.* 329.

On the 4th of March, Queen Anne gave the royal assent to the bill for the union of England and Scotland. These two kingdoms, though united under one king from the days of James I., had maintained their separate Parliaments, and regarded themselves as independent nations.—*Pict. Eng., Vol.* 4, *p.* 178.

The first Parliament of united Great Britain met on the 23d of October.

In the battle of Oudenarde, Marlborough gained another
great victory. This defeat was followed by the loss of
1708. Lisle, Ghent, and Bruges. In Spain the allies were unsuccessful; but at sea they gained some advantages, and took
the islands of Sardinia and Minorca.—*Mod. Europe, Vol.* 2, *pp.*
332–334.

His heavy losses induced Louis to propose peace, but his proposition was rejected, except on terms too humiliating for his acceptance, and he prepared afresh for war.

At Malplaquet, Marlborough again defeated the French, but
with the loss of nearly 20,000 men, the French losing
1709. only 10,000.—*Mod. Europe, Vol.* 2, *p.* 336. *Pict. Eng.,*
Vol. 4, *p.* 216.

Samuel Johnson, the great English essayist, poet, and lexicographer, was born September 18th, this year. A man of great genius and massive talents, his name stands among the foremost in English literature.—*S. Johnson in Am. Cy.*

The queen, who had long since transferred her affections to a
new favorite, now broke all connection with the Duchess
1710. of Marlborough, and, removing her Whig ministers, she

brought in the Tories with Harley, afterwards Earl of Oxford, and St. John, Viscount of Bolingbroke, at their head. The new ministry favored closing the war.—*Mod. Europe, Vol.* 2, *p.* 345. *Pict. Eng., Vol.* 4, *pp.* 225, 226.

David Hume, the historian, was born in Edinburgh, April 26th.
1711. His name is one of the most noted in the literature and philosophy of this century.—*Hume in Am. Cy.*

The age of Queen Anne was as brilliant in literature as it was in arms. Such names as those of Addison, Steele, Swift, Pope, Thomson, Young, and Watts, all writing at this time, gave a rare lustre to her reign.

The Peace of Utrecht, which closed the war of the Spanish Succession left Philip in peacable possession of Spain.
1713. This peace, so far as England was concerned, was the work of the tories, who hated Marlborough, and desired to be rid of the necessity of employing him. The treaty has always been unpopular in England.—*Mod. Europe, Vol.* 2, *p.* 358.

On the 1st of August, Queen Anne died, and was succeeded by George I. of Hanover, whose succession to the Eng-
1714. lish crown had been fixed by act of Parliament, he not being the next heir. Great hopes had been entertained by the friends of the Pretender, that he would be recalled on the death of his sister Anne, but the Whig statesmen took good care to secure the throne to George, and they came into power again with him.—*Pict. Eng., Vol.* 4, *pp.* 280–284. *Smucker's Four Georges, pp.* 33–36.

A strong party in England was in favor of the Pretender, and the narrow-minded and vulgar George, with his Ger-
1715. man attendants, did not help matters much. In Scotland, the Pretender was openly preferred. He was publicly proclaimed king, and a formidable force was raised to seat him on the throne. He landed at Peterhead, December 22d, but after a short time deserted his followers and returned to France.—*Mod. Europe, Vol.* 2, *pp.* 370–373.

To prevent the Jacobites and Tories from gaining power by the elections to a new Parliament, the Septennial bill was
1716. passed, fixing the duration of the terms of the members

of Parliament at seven years instead of three.—*Pict. Eng., Vol. 4, pp.* 309, 310. *Smucker's Four Georges, pp.* 46, 47.

1718. England, the German Empire, Holland, and France, formed the Quadruple Alliance against the ambitious projects of Spain, now controlled by Cardinal Alberoni, the bold and unscrupulous minister of Philip. A war with Spain grew out of this alliance.—*Mod. Europe, Vol.* 2, *p.* 393.

1719. The South Sea scheme occasioned one of the wildest scenes of commercial speculation recorded in history. It was a mamouth company to trade with Spanish South America, and was designed to pay off the immense public debt. The spirit of speculation swept over the country like a tornado. The bubble burst the next year, scattering ruin among all classes.—*Mod. Europe, Vol* 2, *pp.* 395–397.

1721. Sir Robert Walpole, a great Whig statesman, was made First Lord of the Treasury and Premier of the English Cabinet. He was one of the first of those great political leaders in which this century abounded, and who were often the real rulers of the realm. Walpole pursued steadily a peace policy, and remained in power the long time of 21 years.—*Walpole, Robert in Am. Cy.*

1723. Bolingbroke, the former minister of Queen Anne, had fled to France after the accession of George I., charged with treason. He was now pardoned, and, returning, he became one of the leaders of that bitter Tory opposition which fought Walpole and the Whigs through this reign.—*The Four Georges, p.* 68. *Pict. Eng., Vol.* 4, *p.* 362.

On the 10th of July, Sir William Blackstone, the great writer on the English Common Law, was born in London. Adam Smith, the eminent political economist, was born at Kirkcaldy, June 5th. These names are among the most illustrious in the roll of England's great thinkers.—*Am. Cy.*

1727. George I. died, June 11th, on his way to Osnaburg in his beloved Hanover. He was succeeded by his son, George II., a man of many vices and of mercenary spirit. But the real ruler of the kingdom was Walpole, who continued to be retained in power.—*Pict. Eng., Vol.* 4, *pp.* 372–374.

William Cowper, one of the purest of England's poets, was
1731. born, November 15th, at Great Berkhamstead. (Cowper
in Am. Cy.). Up to this date, all law proceedings in England had been written in Latin. The custom was now abolished, but not without great opposition from the lawyers.—*Pict. Eng., Vol.* 4, *p.* 383.

The English ships carried on an illicit but profitable commerce
1738. with the Spanish American Colonies. The Spaniards
justly treated these traders as smugglers and pirates, and made complaints to the English government. Walpole desired to preserve peace by doing justice, but the English mind was roused by the story of the wrongs done to English sailors, and Parliament rocked with stormy debates.—*Pict. Eng., Vol.* 4, *pp.* 405, 406.

The clamor of the opposition at length prevailed, and war was
1739. declared, October 11th, amidst popular rejoicings. Ad-
miral Vernon was immediately sent with a fleet to the West Indies, and Admiral Haddock with another cruised off the coast of Spain.—*Mod. Europe, Vol.* 2, *pp.* 419, 413.

In the war of the Austrian Succession, which broke out in
1741. 1740, England took the side of the Austrian queen,
Maria Theresa, against Frederick II. of Prussia, and Charles Albert of Bavaria. France took sides with Frederick.—*Pict. Eng., Vol.* 4, *pp.* 422, 423. *Kohlrausch's Germany, p.* 378.

The war with Spain was still in progress. Admiral Vernon, with a powerful fleet, attacked Carthagena, in South America, but miserably failed, Commodore Anson led another expedition around Cape Horn, and after many adventures he reached England, in 1744, by the way of the Cape of Good Hope, having circumnavigated the globe.—*Bancroft, Vol.* 3, *p.* 439.

Walpole finally succumbed to the fierce opposition which for
1742. years had battled against him. His enemies, rallying all
their forces, gained a majority, and he resigned.—*The Four Georges, pp.* 136, 137. *Pict. Eng., Vol.* 4, *p.* 431.

England again determined to interfere on the side of Austria,
1743. and George II. resolved to accompany the troops. The
English army met the French near Dettingen, and, by

chance, gained a great victory.—*Four Georges, p.* 141. *Pict. Eng., Vol.* 4, *pp.* 439, 440.

Though English and French fleets and troops had met in hostile array, it was only as allies of other powers. On the
1744. 15th of March, France formally declared war, and the conflagration became general. The two powers were already struggling for America and its rich trade.—*Ban., Vol.* 3, *p.* 450.

On the 11th of May, was fought the battle of Fontenoy, in Belgium. It came near being an English victory, but
1745. it was suddenly turned to a disastrous defeat.—*Fontenoy in Am. Cy.*

The loss of the English at Fontenoy gave courage to the French to fit out another expedition to establish Charles
1746. Edward, the young Pretender, on the throne of his fathers. Charles landed in Scotland in July 1745, took Edinburgh, and, gaining the victory of Preston Pans, advanced into England. He was compelled to retreat, and after many vicissitudes, on the 17th of April, 1746, his forces were utterly routed at Culloden, and he escaped in disguise to the continent.—*Pict. Eng., Vol.* 4, *pp.* 454–511. *Charles Edward in Am. Cy.*

In July, Admiral Anson defeated the French fleet off Cape Finisterre; Admiral Hawke, off Belleisle, captured six
1747. French ships; and several other victories were gained by the English fleets. But the French gained several victories over the English, Dutch, and Austrians in the Netherlands.—*Pict. Eng. Vol.* 4, *p.* 527.

The Peace of Aix la Chapelle restored quiet to Europe, after immense expenditures of life and treasure, and immense
1748. additions to the national debt.—*Bancroft, Vol.* 3, *p.* 466.

The violent animosity which existed between George II. and his eldest son Frederick, Prince of Wales, had greatly
1751. complicated British politics, Frederick being the leader or tool of the opposition party. This bad man and heartless son died the 20th of March.—*Pict. Eng., Vol.* 4, *p.* 537.

The Gregorian Calendar, dating from 1582, had long been in use on the continent. In September, it was, by act of
1752. Parliament, introduced into England, the 3d of Septem-

ber being reckoned as the 14th.—*Calendar in American Cy.*

In the Seven Years' War between Prussia and Austria, which opened this year, England took sides with Prussia, and
1756. France joined Austria. Their colonies in America had already been fighting two years, and the two nations were come to the last deadly grapple for the possession of North America. England had met with some mortifying and disastrous defeats and losses, which compelled the ministry to resign. William Pitt, known as the Great Commoner, afterwards Earl of Chatham, and one of the most eloquent of men, was called to the Premiership. He was dismissed the following April, but was soon recalled. Under his energetic management, England became again successful. The course of the war in America has already been detailed under "America." The events on the continent belong rather to the history of Prussia and Austria than to that of England.—*Pict. Eng., Vol.* 4, *p.* 560. *Bancroft, Vol.* 4, *pp.* 247, 271–276.

The war now raging extended also to the East Indies, and in 1756, the French Indian ally, Surajah Dowlah, had taken
1757. Calcutta, and thrown his prisoners into the famous Black Hole. Lord Clive, a young general of desperate courage, retook Calcutta in January, 1757, drove the French from their settlements, and, on the 23d of June, with 3,000 men, met and defeated the army of Surajah Dowlah, 65,000 strong. This great victory laid the foundations of the great empire of the English in the East Indies.—*Clive in Am. Cy. The Four Georges, pp.* 162–167.

An English force landed on the coast of France, and, with the aid of the English fleet, captured Cherbourg, which, how-
1758. ever, they immediately relinquished, and returned to England. Another force sent soon after was captured or destroyed by the French.—*Pict. Eng. Vol.* 4, *p.* 574.

Admiral Boscawen defeated the French fleet off Cape Lagon. Another great naval victory was gained over the French
1759. by Admiral Hawke, in Quiberon Bay. The battle was fought during a tempestuous storm.—*Pict. Eng., Vol.* 4, *p.* 578.

On the death of George II., October 25, his grandson, George

1760. III., succeeded. The new king was accounted a moderate Whig, and was warmly welcomed to the throne by the English people. Though of arbitrary and obstinate temper, he was a man of pure morals, and the best, by far, of the Hanoverian kings.—*The Four Georges, p.* 168, *and pp.* 180–183.

Pitt retired from the ministry in October, 1761, and in the following April, the Earl of Bute, the incompetent favorite
1762. of the king, became Premier. This change cost George much of his popularity.—*Pict. Eng., Vol.* 4, *p.* 804, *p.* 813. *Pitt and Bute in Am. Cy.*

This year Havana was taken by an English fleet, and the French West Indies fell into the hands of the British.—*Pict. Eng., Vol.* 4, *p.* 809. *Bancroft, Vol.* 4, *p.* 444.

On the 10th of February, was ratified the Peace of Paris, which closed the war between England, France, and
1763. Spain. This peace left England with an immense increase of territory and of power, but with an enormous debt of seven hundred millions of dollars.—*Bancroft, Vol.* 4, *p.* 454, *and p.* 462.

In April, Bute, ridiculed and hated, resigned, and George Grenville became Prime Minister. It was he whose audacity devised the Stamp Act.—*The Four Georges, pp.* 194–196. *Bancroft, Vol.* 5, *pp.* 94, 95.

While the English statesmen were throwing away an empire by their Stamp Acts, James Watt, an English mechan-
1765. ician, gave them a new and richer empire over a great natural power, by the invention of the steam engine. Next to the art of printing, the steam engine has promoted the civilization of mankind.—*Steam engine and Watt in Am. Cy.*

Grenville had been obliged to retire in 1765, and was succeeded by Rockingham as Premier. He, too, soon re-
1766. signed, and William Pitt, who was now made Earl of Chatham, again became Prime Minister. Perhaps he might have allayed the rising storm, but he was disabled from much attention to business, and his collegues were not competent to so grave a task.—*Bancroft, Vol.* 5, *p.* 300, *and Vol.* 6, *pp.* 19–28.

John Wilkes, a member of Parliament, had, in 1763, published

1768. a libellous paper against the government, for which he
was expelled and outlawed, after scenes of furious excitement. He was now elected member from Middlesex, and being refused his seat, he was again and again re-elected, but, finally, his opponent was declared elected, though Wilkes had an overwhelming majority. England was in a whirl of rage and excitement, and a revolution seemed imminent. But American troubles were rising, and this perhaps saved England.—*The Four Georges, pp.* 197–202, *and pp.* 218–220.

Richard Arkwright this year invented the Spinning Jenny, which made it possible to spin cotton into thread suitable for warp. This revolutionized, in after years, the cotton manufacture, and changed, doubtless, the history of the world.—*Arkwright in Am. Cy.*

On the 28th of January, Lord North, who was already in the
Cabinet, became Prime Minister. His ministry is noted
1770. as that under which the American Revolution occurred.
He was the ready tool of George III. He had a powerful opposition to contend with.—*Pict. Eng., Vol.* 4, *pp.* 880, 881.

Samuel Taylor Coleridge, the eminent poet and philosopher,
was born, October 21st, at Ottery St. Mary. He died in
1772. 1834. A man of mighty genius, but of infirm purpose,
he did much, but left undone more which he might easily have accomplished.—*S. T. Coleridge in Am, Cy.*

For the next ten years, England was occupied with the troubles and war which lost her American colonies. This war soon involved her in a war with France and Spain. Parliamentary strifes at home, and great outrages in the East Indies, completed the picture.

The Spaniards, aided by a French fleet, undertook the siege
of Gibraltar. This siege attracted the attention of all
1779. Europe. It was one of the most wonderful sieges in
history. It was practically abandoned in 1782.—*Gibraltar in Am. Cy.*

England having assumed and exercised the right of searching
the vessels of neutral countries to prevent them from
1780. carrying to hostile ports articles contraband of war,

Russia, Prussia, Sweden, and Denmark entered into an Armed Neutrality to protect the rights of neutral vessels, declaring that "free bottoms make free goods."—*Pict. Eng., Vol.* 5, *p.* 317.

This year, Hyder Ali, Sultan of Mysore, invaded the English East Indies, and ravaged with fire and sword.—*H. Ali in Am. Cy.*

The Peace of Versailles, in which England acknowledged the
Independence of the United States, closed also the war
1783. with France and Spain.—*Mod. Europe, Vol.* 3, *p.* 153.

William Pitt, "the younger," was the second son of "the great commoner." He became a member of Parliament at the age of 21, and soon became one of the leaders of the opposition. On the 19th of December, he was made Prime Minister of England, being only a little over 24 years of age. He was one of the ablest parliamentary leaders ever known, and his ministry was one of the stormiest and longest in English history.—*William Pitt in Am. Cy.*

Tippoo Sahib, who succeeded his father, Hyder Ali, December
1784. 7th, 1782, gave, by his military genius, a new impulse to
the war, and gained such advantages, that in March
1784, he concluded a peace on terms highly favorable to himself.
—*Tippoo Sahib in Am. Cy.*

Warren Hastings, the able but rapacious and cruel Governor
1786. General of India, after making peace with Tippoo Sahib,
returned to England, and was impeached in Parliament
for maladministration. This trial, one of the most celebrated in history, terminated, in 1795, with his acquittal. The speeches of Burke, in this trial, are masterpieces of forensic eloquence.—*Hastings in Am. Cy. The Four Georges, pp.* 244–248.

Tippoo Sahib again commenced war against the English by
1790. invading the realms of some of the native princes in alliance with England.—*Tippoo Sahib in Am. Cy. Pict. Eng., Vol.* 5, *p.* 797.

The French Revolution was now raging, and clubs of sympathizers were formed in various places in England. The brilliant Fox, and the eloquent Sheridan, took sides with France, but Burke, disgusted with the violence of the French republicans, denounced them.—*The Four Georges, pp.* 255–257.

Tippoo, after meeting several repulses, was at length besieged in his capital, Seringapatam, and compelled to sue for
1792. peace, which he obtained by giving up half his territories, and paying an immense sum of money.

The monarchs of Europe, alarmed by the spread of the republican ideas from France, formed a coalition against the
1793. French people. England took a leading part in this movement, and sent out its armies and fleets to aid in the suppression of the Revolutionary government. For years England rocked in the waves raised by the storms on the continent, and expended millions in the effort to compel such a peace as she wished.—*Mod. Europe, Vol.* 3, *p.* 326. *Thiers' French Revolution, Vol.* 2, *p.* 84.

The success of the French armies compelled one and another power to withdraw from the coalition within a year or two, and in some countries, the Republican party, aided by France, got the ascendancy, and became allies of the French. England still struggled on, with the indomitable Pitt at the helm, and with the victorious Nelson sweeping the seas.—*Pitt and Nelson in Am. Cy.*

A terrible mutiny broke out among the sailors of the Channel fleet, occasioned by the discontents with the small pay
1797. and the cruel usage allotted to seamen. The mutiny assumed such formidable proportions, the ships were declared in a state of rebellion.—*Pict. Eng., Vol.* 6, *pp.* 111–116. *Mod. Europe, Vol.* 3, *pp.* 404, 406.

The French sent this year an expedition against England. About 1400 troops landed in Wales, and, after wandering about some time, surrendered to a superior force.—*Pict. Eng., Vol.* 6, *p.* 117. *Mod. Europe, Vol.* 3, *p.* 404.

In May, Bonaparte led an expedition into Egypt. Nelson, who was cruising in the Mediterranean, followed, and in
1798. the Battle of the Nile, fought August 1st and 2d, almost totally destroyed the French fleet.—*Pict. Eng., Vol.* 6, *p.* 136. *Thiers' Rev., Vol.* 4, *p.* 286.

An Irish rebellion, fomented by the French government, broke out on the 23d of May. A small French force succeeded in landing, but was beaten and surrendered, and the rebellion was suppressed as all other Irish rebellions had been.—*Pict. Eng.*, *Vol.* 6, *pp.* 127, 128. *Thiers' Rev.*, *Vol.* 4, *pp.* 306, 307. *Mod. Europe*, *Vol.* 3, *pp.* 406–408.

In this summer, a second coalition was formed by the efforts of Austria and England, against Republican France, and war was again speedily raging over Europe.—*Thiers' Rev.*, *Vol.* 4, *p.* 292, *and pp.* 308–317.

1800. In January 1799, the Parliament proposed and passed some resolutions as a basis of union between England and Ireland. In February 1800, the Irish Parliament acceded to the terms, and the union was consummated. A bitter opposition to the measure existed in Ireland, and it was charged that bribery and corruption had been resorted to, to carry the measure. The Irish still hate the union, and sigh for independence.—*Pict. Eng.*, *Vol.* 6, *p.* 138, *and p.* 148. *Mod. Europe*, *Vol.* 3, *p.* 419.

The century closed over England still at war with France, and struggling obstinately to resist the great over-mastering genius who then led the French nation.

FRANCE.

Louis XIV., hated, feared, and admired, was still on the French throne when the Eighteenth Century dawned. He had lost most of the great men who had helped to give success to his arms and wisdom to his councils, and his people were impoverished and exhausted by his immense wars; but he was still arrogant and restless, and was girding himself for that last great struggle by which he hoped to unite the throne of Spain to that of France.

The century was a brilliant though a sad one for France. It found her under the despotic hand of Louis *le Grand*. It left her in the iron grasp of the greater Napoleon, with a century of sins and sorrows and blood stretching between them. Endless wars, reckless extravagance, insane debaucheries, at last produced their effects, and France paid in tears and blood for the sins of centuries.

In the year 1700, Philip of Anjou, the grandson of Louis XIV., and, by his mother's side, grandson of Philip IV. of
1702. Spain, was proclaimed as Philip V., by virtue of the will of his uncle, the childless Charles II. Charles of Austria, another grandson of Philip IV., also claimed the crown. Both parties prepared for war. Philip was supported chiefly by France, and Charles, by England, Holland, and his father, the emperor Leopold. Several other powers afterwards took sides with one party or the other, while Spain itself was divided, the larger part supporting Philip. But the chief parties in the contest were France and England; and the real point at issue was the aggrandizement of France by the ultimate union of France and Spain. A few successes were gained in 1702 and 1703 by the English and their allies, in Italy and Netherlands; and some by the French in Bavaria, and on the Rhine.—*Mod. Europe, Vol.* 2, *pp.* 309, 310. *White's France, pp.* 378, 379.

The French penetrated into Germany to the Danube, where, August 13th, they were met by the armies of Marl-
1704. borough and Eugene, and defeated in the great battle of Blenheim. The French lost their commanding general and 40,000 men. This was the first great pitched battle lost by the armies of Louis, and it broke the spell of his power. It was hailed by Europe as the hour of deliverance from a long thralldom.—*Mod. Europe, Vol.* 2, *p.* 314.

On the 23d of May, the French suffered another great defeat
1706. at Ramillies in Belgium. In Spain, the French lost Barcelona, and were driven from Maderia; and in Italy they suffered severe reverses, and were compelled to relinquish most of their possessions. Louis was so far humbled by these successive defeats and disasters, that he offered liberal terms of peace; but the English and allies, rendered haughty by success, rejected these terms, and proposed others so severe, that Louis could not, with honor, accept them. He therefore prepared to renew the conflict.—*Mod. Europe, Vol.* 2, *pp.* 325, 326.

Louis still continued unfortunate in Italy; but in Spain, the French won, April 25th, a great and decisive victory on
1707. the plains of Almanza, which firmly established Philip on his throne.—*Mod. Europe, Vol.*, 2, *p.* 329.

The French, rallying fresh armies, invaded Belgium, and were met and again heavily beaten by Marlborough, in the
1708. Battle of Oudenarde, fought July 8th, This was followed by the siege of Lisle, by the fall of which France lay again exposed to its foes.—*Mod. Europe, Vol.* 2, *pp.* 332, 333.

Again Louis sought terms of peace. A winter of terrible severity had produced famine in his kingdom, and the
1709. poor old king offered to relinquish Spain, to drive out the English Pretender, and to agree to nearly all the terms required of him; but the allies, flushed with victory, added to their terms, and Louis, in despair, appealed to his people, who rallied promptly to his support. Another great French army took the field. Retribution was following on the path of this old oppressor of the nations, and, at Malplaquet, his armies were again beaten, though with a much heavier loss to the allies than to the French. The French armies gained some new advantages in Spain.—*Mod. Europe, Vol.* 2, *pp.* 335, 336.

The change of parties in England, and the accession of Charles to the throne of the empire, saved France. Europe did not care to see the imperial crown and that of Spain united on the same head, and Philip's right to Spain was finally acknowledged on his resigning all claims to the crown of France. Hostilities continued for some months, especially in America.

The Peace of Utrecht closed the great European war of the Spanish Succession—a war which broke the power of
1713. France, and loaded both France and England with gigantic debts.—*Mod. Europe, Vol.* 2, *pp.* 347–358.

On the 1st of September, Louis XIV. died, after a reign of 72 years, and was succeeded by his great grandson, Louis
1715. XV., a boy of five years.—*Louis XIV. and Louis XV. in Am. Cy.*

Fenelon, the amiable and excellent author of Telemaque, and tutor to the grandsons of Louis XIV., died this year.

France became a party to the Quadruple Alliance, which was
1718. formed to resist the designs of conquest developed by
Alberoni, the ambitious minister of Philip V.—*Mod. Europe, Vol.* 2, *p.* 393.

John Law, a Scotch adventurer, proposed, as a plan of paying off the national debt of France, a company for working the mines supposed to exist on the banks of the Mississippi. The stock of the Company suddenly rose to fabulous prices. France ran wild with the hopes of exhaustless wealth. The bubble burst in 1720, filling the nation with ruin and distress.—*White's France, pp.* 390, 391.

To resist the schemes of Alberoni, a French army was sent
1719. over the Pyrenees, which captured St. Sebastian and
Fontarabia.

Cardinal Fleury, an aged priest, was made Prime Minister.
1726. He earnestly sought to maintain peace with all Europe,
and patronized sciences and the arts in France.—*Fleury in Am. Cy.*

Louis XV. had married the daughter of Stanislaus, a deposed
king of Poland, and on the vacation of the Polish throne,
1733. by the death of Augustus II., France and Spain supported Stanislaus' claim—whence arose the so-called war of the Polish Succession. Germany supported the claims of Augustus III. of Saxony.

The French invaded and conquered Lorraine, then a German
duchy, and besieged and took Philipsburg.—*Mod. Eu-*
1734. *rope, Vol.* 2, *p.* 402.

The emperor was at length driven to desire peace, and, with
the concurrence of the peace-loving Cardinal Fleury, the
1735. Treaty of Vienna was made, in which Stanislaus received the duchy of Lorraine in place of his lost kingdom, and Francis of Lorraine became Grand Duke of Tuscany.—*Stanislaus I. and Louis XV. in Am. Cy. Mod. Europe, Vol.* 2, *p.* 402.

In the great war of the Austrian Succession, which broke out
in 1740, France took sides with Bavaria and Prussia,
1743. and French armies advanced into Germany. In the battle of Dettingen, fought June 27th, the French, by the blunder

of one of their generals, were defeated with great loss.—*Modern Europe, Vol.* 2, *p.* 420, *p.* 428.

England having taken sides with Austria, the English and French forces and fleets frequently came into collision,
1744. and the French government, in conjunction with Spain, openly declared war against England and Austria.—*Mod. Europe, Vol.* 2, *pp.* 430, 431.

For the several events of this war, see dates under "England." The Peace of Aix la Chapelle closed the war, and restored tranquility to Europe and America.

During this half century a brilliant set of writers were busy filling France with new and often dangerous ideas.
1750. Partaking of the laxity of morals of a most licentious court, and disgusted with a Christianity whose only representatives were the debauched and greedy ecclesiastics of the times, they ridiculed religion, and undermined all the foundations of good order and law. Their words were the winged seeds of revolution and anarchy, which, in later years, bore bitter fruits. —*France (Language and Literature) in Am. Cy. Thiers' Rev., Introduction, pp.* V.–VII.

Louis XV., at the outset, a model of virtue and purity in his family, afterwards became debauched and profligate.
1753. About this date, Madame Pompadour, one of his mistresses, obtained complete control over him, and was virtually ruler of France. Thus, through war, infidelity, and licentiousness, France hastened to its doom.—*Louis XV. and Madame Pompadour in Am. Cy.*

The French government now engaged in that last terrible grapple for the possession of North America. For the
1754. events of this war, see dates under "America" and "England."—*White's France. pp.* 409–411.

The so-called *Family Compact* was formed between the Bourbon kings of France, Spain, and Naples, to guarantee
1761. each other's possessions, and agreeing to count an enemy of either as the enemy of all.—*Pict. Eng., Vol.* 4, *p.* 804. *White's France, p.* 411.

At the Peace of Paris, which closed the war, France ceded

1763. Canada and most of Louisiana, with many other places,
to England, and received back her East India possessions.—*Mod. Europe, Vol. 2, p.* 576.

The Jesuits, by their rapid growth and arts, had attained im-
1764. mense power, which was often exerted for selfish and
sinister ends. Their power and great possessions awakened the jealousy of kings and cabinets. In this year they were expelled from France.—*White's France, p.* 412. *Jesuits in Am. Cy.*

Stanislaus, after a wise and beneficent reign, died, and Lor-
1766. raine, as had been before stipulated, became a portion of
France.—*Stanislaus in Am. Cy.*

Napoleon Bonaparte, the greatest military chief, and, in many
1769. respects, the greatest genius of modern times, was born,
August 15th, in Ajaccio, in Corsica, about two months after this island had relinquished its struggle for independence, and become a part of France.—*White's France, p.* 413.

On the 10th, of May, Louis XV., after a long and dishonorable
1774. reign of 59 years, died, exhausted, hated, and despised,
and was succeeded by his grandson, the unfortunate Louis XVI., an amiable but awkward young man of twenty years, who, four years before, had married Marie Antoinette, daughter of the emperor of Germany.—*Louis XVI. in Am. Cy.*

Louis made the aged Maurepas Prime Minister, and Turgot, an honest and talented man, Minister of Finance. But it was beyond human skill to rescue the finances of the kingdom from their hopeless disorder.—*White's France, pp.* 419–421.

Turgot's proposed reforms awakened against him great opposi-
1776. tion, and he was soon superseded by Necker, who had
been a banker at Geneva. Necker also attempted reform; but the corrupt nobility steadily opposed every measure which threatened to impose any part of the burden of taxation upon them. France was full of violence and distress.—*Necker in Am. Cy. White's France, p.* 422.

Necker, persevering in his plans, increased the resources of
1781. the crown, and diminished the expenditures; but the
opposition at length compelled him to resign. He was

succeeded by Calonne, whose foolish measures only increased the troubles.—*Necker in Am. Cy.*

The part which France took in the American Revolution plunged her into a war with England. This war was
1783. closed by the Peace of Versailles.— *White's France, p.* 428.

The Parliament of Paris, refusing to concur in the measures proposed by the minister, Calonne, was banished to
1787. Troyes. Nearly a month later, Louis recalled this Parliament, but the rising spirit of revolution was not quelled; the storm was ready to burst.—*Thiers' French Rev. Vol.* 1, *p.* 22.

Necker was loudly called for by the people, and being recalled to the ministry, he seconded the general cry for the as-
1788. sembling of the States-General. This being resolved on, all minds turned to its anticipated meeting as to the last hope for the disorders of the State.—*Thiers' Rev., Vol.* 1, *p.* 27.

French Revolution. On the 5th of May, the States-General assembled, composed of nearly 1,200 members, dele-
1789. gates from the nobility, the clergy, and the Tiers-etat, or the people. The nobility and clergy insisted upon sitting upon and deliberating on the Tiers-etat, each in its own chamber. The Tiers-etat refused to be counted a separate body, and after waiting till the 17th of June, and inviting the nobles and clergy to meet with them, they declared themselves *The National Assembly*, and assumed the control of affairs. The Revolution was begun.—*Thiers' Rev., Vol.* 1, *pp.* 39–46.

On the 14th of July, the populace of Paris, arming themselves, stormed the Bastile, a State prison and citadel, which had grown hateful from its having been an instrument of tyranny, and put the commandant to death. All Paris—all France—was at once in the most violent commotion. The world never before witnessed scenes so full of insane excitement and terror. Events crowded upon each other in quick and frightful succession.—*Thiers' Rev., Vol.* 1, *pp.* 66–70. *White's France, p.* 434.

The republican spirit grew rapidly, and, on June 19th, titles of nobility were abolished by a decree of the National
1790. Assembly.—*Thiers' Rev., Vol.* 1, *p.* 150.

July 14th, the anniversary of the storming of the Bastile, a grand fete of Federation was held. Delegates from all the provinces were present. The king and nation took, amid magnificent ceremonies, the oath of fidelity to the Constitution. The sunshine was of short duration; the tempest soon returned.—*Thiers' Rev., Vol.* 1, *pp.* 151–154.

Mirabeau, a bold, bad man of over-mastering talents and influence, and the leader of the National Assembly, died,
1791. April 2d. No one seemed able after him to control the storm.—*Thiers' Rev., Vol.* 1, *pp.* 172–174.

June 21st, the king, terrified at the prospect, fled from Paris, but was arrested at Varennes, and carried back a prisoner.—*Thiers' Rev., Vol.* 1, *pp.* 176–181.

On the 30th of September, the National Constituent Assembly dissolved, and on the next day, the new National Legislative Assembly met.—*Thiers' Rev., Vol.* 1, *p.* 193.

With the Legislative Assembly, there came two new parties, the Girondists, a party of brilliant talents, and, in theory,
1792. moderate Republicans; and the Mountain, a party of fierce radical Democrats. The Girondists soon had a majority. *Thiers' Rev., Vol.* 1, *pp.* 198–201.

Large numbers of the old nobility had fled from France, and these emigrants, as they were called, assembled chiefly at Coblentz, to watch their opportunity to resume power. Austria and Prussia were in arms to suppress the revolution. These movements kindled still higher the flames. August 10th, the palace was stormed by the mob, and the king and family, fleeing to the Assembly, were thrown into prison.—*Thiers' Rev., Vol.* 1, *pp.* 320–330.

September 2d to the 6th, occurred the terrible butchery of the inmates of the several prisons in Paris.—*Thiers.*

This was a year of horrors. January 21st, Louis XVI. was guillotined.—*Thiers' Rev., Vol.* 2, *p.* 77.

1793. All Europe was shocked and alarmed, and the First Coalition of the hostile monarchs was formed to suppress the terrible Republic. In La Vendee, an insurrection of Royalists broke out, and became the celebrated Vendean War, which lasted several years.—*Thiers' Rev., Vol.* 2, *p.* 150.

The Mountain increased in power. On the 2d of June, the Girondists fell, and twenty-two were sent to prison.—*Thiers' Rev., Vol.* 2, *pp.* 189–193.

The Reign of Terror became universal.

July 13th, Charlotte Corday, a frantic enthusiast, assassinated Marat, the editor of a most atrocious paper, and one of the most malevolent of the revolutionists. Robespierre now ruled without a rival. Revolutionary tribunals were erected, and France swam in blood.—*Thiers' Rev., Vol.* 2, *p.* 229. *White's France, pp.* 444, 445.

War raged on all the borders of France, but nothing could withstand the insane energy of the Republican armies.—*Thiers' Revolution.*

On the 28th of July, Robespierre, having fallen under popular disfavor, was beheaded on the same spot where he had
1794. sacrificed so many thousands, and the "Reign of Terror" came to an end.—*Thiers' Rev., Vol.* 3, *pp.* 104, 105.

During these years of terror, France was meeting, with almost super-human energy, the armies of the Coalition which menaced all her borders. Great victories were won, and France was repeatedly saved. General Pichegru especially gained many laurels.—*White's France, pp.* 447–451.

On the 26th of October, the Legislative Assembly was dissolved, after adopting a Constitution, creating a Council
1795. of Five Hundred, a Council of Ancients, and a Directory of Five Directors.—*Thiers' Rev., Vol.* 3, *pp.* 332, 333.

October 5th, the mob of Paris attempted the old game of insurrections, but the grape-shot of Napoleon Bonaparte soon brought them to their senses.—*Thiers' Rev., Vol.* 3, *p.* 325.

October 27th, the new government came into power, and, on the 1st of November, the Directory was formed.—*Thiers' Rev., Vol.* 3, *p.* 334, *p.* 338.

Bonaparte was appointed to the command of the army of Italy, and entered upon that wonderful career of victory and
1796. power which soon filled the world with his name. Marching over the Alps, and descending into the plain of Italy, victory followed victory in rapid succession. May 9th, Bona-

parte forced the terrible passage of the bridge of Lodi, and, on the 15th, took possession of Milan.—*White's France, pp.* 465, 466. *Thiers' Rev., Vol.* 3, *pp.* 405, 406.

The victorious career of Bonaparte continued till all northern
Italy, falling into his hands, was erected into the Cis-
1797. alpine Republic. France seemd to think it her mission
to make all Europe Republican.—*Thiers' Vol.* 4, *p.* 217,

February 10th, the French entered Rome, and shortly after
abolished the Papal government, and proclaimed the
1798. Roman Republic.

Bonaparte, led by the mere love of glory, next conducted an expedition to Egypt, and won a victory over the Mamelukes near the Pyramids.

The French invasion of Ireland, and the English invasion of France, and also the Second Coalition, were noted under "England."

With foes on all her borders, winning victories, France was
again ready to fall into civil convulsions. Bonaparte, in
1799. this crisis, interfered, overturned the Constitution, and
under another Constitution, was himself made First Consul and virtual ruler of France.—*White's France, pp.* 475, 476. *Thiers' Rev., Vol.* 4, *pp.* 425–429.

The First Consul, putting himself at the head of his troops,
soon turned the tide of victory against the armies of the
1800. Second Coalition. In May, he scaled and crossed the
Alps. June 14th, he met the Austrian forces on the plain of Marengo, and after being nearly defeated, won a great victory, which restored Italy to the French control.—*White's France, pp.* 479, 480.

The victory of Hohenlinden, won on the Rhine, December 3d, by Moreau, completed the triumph of France over the Coalition. Thus the century closed over France, robbed of her liberties, but covered with military glory.

SPAIN AND PORTUGAL.

The Seventeenth Century closed in Spain with the death of Charles II., the last of the Hapsburgs, and the accession of Philip V., the first of the Bourbons. The long war of the Spanish Succession, which finally left Philip firmly seated on his throne, belonged more to France and England than to Spain. Its greatest battles were fought in Germany and Netherlands, and not in Spain. At the Peace of Utrecht, Spain was compelled to cede Naples, Sardinia, Parma, Milan, and the Spanish Netherlands to Austria, Sicily to Savoy, and Gibraltar and Minorca to England. Philip secured simply Spain and Spanish possessions in America. The events of the War of the Spanish Succession have already been detailed under "England" and "France."

Portugal, which shook off the Spanish yoke in 1640, was, at the opening of the Eighteenth Century, under Pedro II., of the House of Braganza. In the war of the Spanish Succession, Portugal took part with England against France. Portugal held, across the water, the great empire of Brazil, rich in mines, and, under her successive monarchs, John V., 1706, and Joseph Emanuel, 1750, continued to prosper.

Cardinal Alberoni, the ambitious minister of the indolent and imbecile Philip V., thought to restore Spain to its former

1718. greatness. He again seized Sardinia and Sicily, and planned the restoration of the Stuarts to England, and the seizure of the regency of France. The alarmed powers formed the Quadruple Alliance, and, after a successful war, compelled the dismission of Alberoni.—*Philip V. and Alberoni in Am. Cy. Mod. Europe, Vol. 2, pp.* 392–394.

Philip, having dismissed Alberoni, acceded to the Quadruple Alliance, and restored Sardinia and Sicily.—*Philip V.*

1720. *in Am. Cy.*

Philip took part with France in the war of the Polish Succession, and sent his son, Don Carlos, with an army into
1733. Italy.—*Mod. Eu., Vol. 2, p.* 402. *Philip V. in Am. Cy.*

The pacification of Vienna, which closed the war of the Polish Succession, gave to Don Carlos the crown of Naples and
1735. Sicily in exchange for the Duchy of Parma, which he had before held.—*Mod. Europe, Vol. 2, p.* 402.

To guard its American possessions from the visits of the English smugglers, Spain stationed ships along the coast,
1739. which not only arrested the smugglers, but often injured the crews of honest traders. England demanded indemnification, and Spain agreed to pay 95,000 pounds sterling. But the right of search still remained an open question, and Spain failing to pay the stipulated sum, England declared war. Large armaments were fitted out by both nations. The events of the war have been noticed under "England."—*Mod. Europe, Vol. 2, pp.* 412–417.

This war was soon merged in the greater war of the Austrian Succession.

Philip V. died, July 9th, after a reign of considerable glory, due rather to his wives than to himself. He was suc-
1746. ceeded by his son Ferdinand VI., his son, Don Carlos, by his second wife, being king of Naples, and another son, Philip, becoming soon after Duke of Parma, thus filling three thrones with Bourbons.—*Philip V. in Am. Cy. Mod. Europe, Vol. 2, p.* 458.

The Peace of Aix la Chapelle, which closed the war of the Austrian Succession, and also the war between Spain
1748. and England, left affairs in the state they were before the war. Even the right of search was left an unsettled point.—*Bancroft, Vol. 3, p.* 466. *Mod. Europe, Vol. 2, p.* 368.

Ferdinand VI., dying without children, was succeeded by his half brother, Don Carlos as Charles III., who, on assum-
1759. ing the crown of Spain, left that of Naples to his son, who became Ferdinand IV., and enjoyed a long and eventful reign.—*Sicilies and Spain in Am. Cy.*

Charles III., having become a party to the Bourbon Family

Compact, was plunged into the war then in progress
1761. between England and France. The arms of Spain were unfortunate, and, at the Peace of Paris in 1763, Charles III. was obliged to yield up Minorca and Florida to Great Britain, and to buy back Havana and the parts of Cuba captured by the English.—*Mod. Europe, Vol.* 2, *p.* 576.

Charles III. joined France in the war she was waging against England in behalf of the American Colonies, and under-
1779. took the siege of Gibraltar. Spanish fleets were also sent to the American seas, but fortune was against Spain.—*Pict. Eng., Vol.* 5, *p.* 279. *Mod. Europe, Vol.* 3, *d.* 128.

After immense expenditures of lives and treasures, the siege of Gibraltar was relinquished. In the Peace of Ver-
1782. sailles, which closed the war, Spain received back Minorca and Florida, but was obliged to leave the coveted rock of Gibraltar in the hands of England.—*Mod. Europe, Vol.* 3, *p.* 153. *Pict. Eng., Vol.* 5, *p.* 390, *p.* 393.

On the death of Charles III., he was succeeded by his son, Charles IV., who soon fell under the influence of
1788. Manuel Godoy, the favorite of his wife.—*Charles IV. in Am. Cy.*

Spain joined the first Coalition against France, but, in 1795, Godoy concluded the Peace of Basel with the French,
1793. and, the next year, entered into a league, offensive and defensive, with them. This alliance involved Spain in a war with England. In 1797, the Spanish fleet was defeated off Cape St. Vincent. Minorca and Trinidad were occupied, and all the ports of Spain were blockaded. The distress compelled Godoy to resign, though he still maintained great power.—*Spain in Am. Cy. Mod. Europe, Vol.* 3, *p.* 403.

GERMANY.

THE old German Empire was rapidly losing its coherency and power when the Eighteenth Century dawned upon Europe. The emperors from the House of Hapsburg or Austria had constantly struggled to increase their patrimonial dominions. From being, in their own right, simple arch-dukes of Austria, they had become also kings of Hungary and Bohemia, and included in their possessions, Styria, Carinthia, Transylvania, Wallachia, Carniola, the Tyrol, and the Austrian Netherlands. But while their power as Austrians increased, their authority as emperors of Germany diminished. The blood of the Thirty Years' War had nearly dissolved the ties that bound the States of Germany together, and several of the larger States, as Prussia, Saxony, Bavaria, and Hanover, aspired to a separate and distinct place among the leading powers of Europe. Leopold I. still wore the imperial crown at the opening of the Eighteenth Century, and true to his house, he was preparing to maintain the power of the Hapsburgs by securing the throne of Spain to his second son Charles. For the war of the Spanish Succession, see proper dates under "England" and "France."

Joseph I. succeeded, on the death of his father, Leopold I., to the crown of Austria, and the throne of the empire. He

1705. determined to continue the war in favor of his brother Charles for the Spanish throne.—*Kohlrausch's Germany, p.* 368.

Joseph died on the 17th of April, and was succeeded by his brother, Charles VI. This changed at once the aspects

1711. of the question of the Spanish Succession. The European powers did not care to add the crown of Spain to that of Germany. Charles had also lost all he had gained in Spain. France was thoroughly humbled, and all parties desired peace.—*Kohlrausch p.* 372.

The Peace of Utrecht took from Charles his hope of the Spanish throne, but gave him the Spanish Netherlands,
1713. Milan, Sardinia, Naples, Mantua, and the seaports of Tuscany.—*Charles VI. in Am. Cy.*

Charles was not a party to the Peace of Utrecht; but the next year he concluded with Spain and Germany the
1714. Peace of Radstadt, and ended the war.

The emperor, having no sons, devoted the remainder of his long reign to securing the Austrian possessions to his daughter, Maria Theresa, who had married Francis, Duke of Lorraine. He drew up for this purpose a solemn decree, called the Pragmatic Sanction, and by various expedients and concessions, secured to it the assent of all the leading powers of the empire and of Europe.—*Kohlrausch p.* 374. *Charles VI. in Am. Cy.*

The Turks had, in 1716, again commenced hostilities, and seized Morea, in Greece. The emperor sent against
1717. them the celebrated Eugene of Savoy, then residing at Vienna. He defeated them at Peterwardein, August 5th, 1716, with great slaughter, and the next year beseiged and captured Belgrade. The Turks made peace the next year.—*Mod. Europe, Vol.* 2, *p.* 392. *Abbott's Austria, pp.* 360–364.

In the war of the Polish Succession, the emperor supported the claims of Augustus III. In this war he lost Lor-
1733. raine, and his son-in-law, the Duke of Lorraine, was made Grand Duke of Tuscany.—*Kohlrausch, p.* 375.

October 26th, Charles VI. died, and Maria Theresa, by the Pragmatic Sanction, took possession of the Austrian
1740. dominions. But the Pragmatic Sanction did not prevent a number of claimants arising for the whole or parts of her territories. Charles Albert of Bavaria was the principal claimant. Frederick II. of Prussia, who had just succeeded to the throne and the splendid army of his father, demanded Silesia, and marched into that province to secure possession. This opened the great European war of the Austrian Succession. France took sides with Bavaria, while England supported Austria.—*Kohl., pp.* 375–377. *Mod. Europe, Vol.* 2, *pp.* 417, 418.

Frederick and his Prussians met the Austrians at Molwitz,

April 10th, and, after a severe battle of four hours, routed
1741. them. This was Frederick's first battle. Two French
armies advanced into Germany, and the affairs of Austria looked
hopeless.—*Kohlrausch. pp*, 377, 378.

Charles Albert of Bavaria was elected emperor of Germany
as Charles VII. But Maria Theresa, a woman of in-
1742. domitable spirit, did not relinquish her rights. Rallying
her faithful Hungarians, she sent an army into Bavaria, and captured Munich, his capital, the very day he was being crowned at Frankfort.—*Kohlrausch, p.* 379.

The Austrians suffering another defeat at the hands of Frederick, Maria Theresa concluded with him the treaty of Breslau, yielding to him the upper and lower Silesia, and agreeing to remain neutral in the war.—*Mod. Europe, Vol.* 2, *p.* 423. *Kohlrausch, p.* 379. *Abbott's Austria, pp.* 435, 436.

The withdrawal of Frederick left the burden of the war to fall
upon the French, who were soon driven out of Bohemia,
1743. and England sending over a new force, the Battle of
Dettingen was fought, June 27th. See under "England."

The successes of Austria alarmed Frederick for the safety of
his acquisitions. He was also strongly solicited by
1744. France to declare war, and, assembling a force of 100,-
000 men, he marched into Bohemia, and took Prague, but was soon driven back with great losses.—*Kohlrausch, p.* 380. *Mod. Europe, Vol.* 2, *p.* 435.

Charles VII. died, January 20th, and Maria Theresa made a
treaty with his son, Maximilian, guaranteeing his posses-
1745. sions, he, in turn, relinquishing all claims to the Austrian
Succession. In September, her husband was chosen emperor as Francis I. But France and Spain with Prussia determined to continue the contest. On the 11th of May, the Battle of Fontenoy was fought, and the French gained a great and decisive victory. France and Spain also sent a strong army over the Alps to attack the Austrian possessions in Italy.—*Abbott's Austria, p.* 452.

On the 3d of June, Frederick gained the victory of Hohenfriedberg. Later, he gained other victories, and took Dresden, where a peace was concluded between Austria and Prussia.—*Kohlrausch, p.* 381. *Fred. II. in Am. Cy.. Abbott's Austria, p.* 454, *p.* 458.

The Peace of Aix la Chapelle, signed October 18th, closed the war between Austria, France, Spain, and England also,
1748. and restored peace to Europe. It confirmed Silesia to Frederick, and the high-spirited Maria Theresa was compelled to give up her Italian conquests.—*Mod. Europe, Vol.* 2, *p.* 467. *Abbott's Austria, p.* 461.

John Wolfgang von Goethe, the greatest of German poets and writers, was born at Frankfort on the Main, August
1749. 28th, and died March 22d, 1832. His name marks an era of the highest intellectual culture in Germany. At ten years of age he wrote in several languages, and meditated poems, and invented stories. His genius was of the most comprehensive character, and of dazzling brightness.—*Goethe in Am. Cy.*

It was evident to all parties that another contest must soon come. The haughty queen of Hungary could not forgive Frederick, nor endure the loss of Silesia. Europe was full of plottings and counter-plots. Austria formed an alliance with France, and England made friends with Prussia. The queen secretly prepared to sieze her lost territories, and engaged Saxony and Russia to assist her.—*Bancroft, Vol.* 4, *pp.* 277–280.

Frederick determined to anticipate the blow, and opened the Seven Years' War, by advancing, in August, with 70,000
1756. men, into Saxony. October 1st, he defeated at Lowositz the imperial army sent against him, and, soon afterwards, the entire Saxon army, 14,000 strong, capitulated.—*Frederick II. in Am. Cy. Kohl., pp.* 383, 384. *Abbott's Austria, pp.* 467–469.

The great powers of Europe were now in arms against Prussia, and Frederick's destruction seemed sure. But he did
1757. not falter. Pouring into Bohemia, he gained, May 6th, the great victory of Prague, but with the cost of over 12,000 men. On the 18th of June, he fought and lost the battle of Kolin, and was compelled to abandon Bohemia.—*Kohlrausch, pp.* 386–388. *Mod. Europe, Vol.* 2, *pp.* 499–502.

The Russians advancing into Prussia met a Prussian army at

Gross Jagerndorf, and defeated it. The French armies from the west entered Hanover, defeated the English forces, and compelled them to agree to disband their troops. The Swedes overran Pomerania. November 5th, Frederick, with 22,000 men, met the French, 60,000 strong, at Rosbach, and, in less than half an hour, completely defeated them. On the 18th, the Austrians gained a victory over a Prussian army at Breslau. December 5th, Frederick attacked the Austrians at Leuthen, and gained another great victory, capturing 21,000 men and 130 cannon. He afterwards recaptured Breslau, and saved Silesia. Thus closed this sanguinary year. Prussia was saved.—*Kohlrausch, pp.* 389–392. *Bancroft, Vol.* 4, *pp.* 284–289.

Frederick's General, Ferdinand of Brunswick, chased the
1758. French out of Germany, defeating them at Crevelt, June 23d. Frederick himself assaulted and captured Schweidnitz, April 18th. On the 24th of August, he met the Russians at Zorndorf, and after one of the bloodiest battles of all his wars, he gained a great victory.—*Kohlrausch, pp.* 393, 394. *Mod. Europe, Vol.* 2, *pp.* 516–519.

The Austrians, on the 14th of October, surprised and routed the right wing of the Prussian army at Hochkirchen.—*Kohl., p.* 394.

All parties rallied with fresh energy for this campaign. August 1st, Ferdinand of Brunswick met the French at
1759. Minden, and defeated them. August 12th, Frederick met the Russians and Austrians at Kunersdorf, and after gaining great advantages, was finally miserably defeated. He afterwards lost Dresden, and, a little later, an army of 13,000 men.—*Kohlrausch, pp.* 398–400.

Frederick still continued unfortunate, and his means seemed nearly exhausted. But his indomitable spirit rose tri-
1760. umphant over all difficulties. At length he gained a victory which enabled him to recover Silesia. November 3d, was fought the bloody battle of Torgau, which gave back Saxony to the Prussians.—*Kohlrausch. pp.* 402–404.

The years 1761 and 1762 were marked with more misfortunes for Prussia, and Silesia was lost; but on the accession of Peter

III. to the throne of Russia, he concluded a peace with Frederick, as did also Sweden, and the Prussians were left free to grapple with Austria. Several victories were gained, and both parties being well exhausted, an armistice was agreed on.—*Frederick II. in Am. Cy.*

The Peace of Hubertsburg closed this terrible war. Maria
Theresa finally relinquished Silesia, to become a perma-
1763. nent component of Prussia. Poor Germany had again
been made the battle field of Europe, and all for nought.—*Kohlrausch, pp.* 406, 407. *Frederick II. in Am. Cy.*

Joseph II. succeeded his father, Francis I., as emperor of Germany. He was the second emperor of the House of
1765. Lorraine, but the imperial title was little more than an
empty name. His mother, the talented Maria Theresa, still ruled in the Austrian dominions.—*Joseph II. in Am. Cy.*

Frederick II. and Maria Theresa became parties with Catherine of Russia to the first partition of Poland. Frederick
1772. took Polish Prussia, except the towns of Thorn and
Dantzic, and a part of Great Poland. Maria Theresa secured as her share Red Russia, a part of Podolia, and a part of Little Poland, between the Vistula and Carpathian mountains.—*Poland in Am. Cy.*

Maximilian Joseph of Bavaria dying without issue, the emperor
Joseph claimed the inheritance, and entered Bavaria with
1778. an army to take possession. The elector-palatine, who
had succeeded Maximilian, consented to yield two-thirds of the territory. Frederick II. took sides against Joseph, and both parties prepared for battle.—*Kohlrausch, p.* 414.

The Peace of Teschen ended the war, which had been confined to a few slight skirmishes, and restored most of
1779. Bavaria to the proper heirs. This was the war of the
Bavarian Succession.—*Kohlrausch, p.* 415.

Joseph II. died, February 20th, after a reign of twenty-five
years. After the death of his mother, in 1780, he had
1790. attempted great reforms in his several dominions, with
the purpose of consolidating them into a more united monarchy. These reforms produced intense dissatisfaction in several pro-

vinces, and consequent revolts. He was succeeded by his brother, Leopold II.—*Joseph II. in Am. Cy. Kohl., pp.* 415–417.

On the death of Leopold, he was succeeded by his son, Francis II., the last emperor of Germany, and the first of the em-

1792. pire of Austria. Germany, and Europe even, were rocking in the wild storm of the French Revolution when he came to the throne, and Austria was especially involved by its efforts to save Maria Antoinette, who was a sister of Joseph and Leopold. —*Francis II. in Am. Cy.*

The Austrians and Prussians combined and marched into France, capturing several towns, and threatening Paris, but on the 5th of November, they suffered a decisive defeat at Jemappes, which lost to Austria all her possessions in the Netherlands.—*Kohlrausch, pp.* 418, 419. *Allison's Europe, Vol.* 1, *pp.* 186–194.

Austria joined the First Coalition, and the allies gained several important victories. But, in 1794, after gaining the

1793. victory of Cateau Cambresis, they were every where repulsed, and, on the 22d May, were defeated by Pichegru, near Tournay.—*Kohlrausch, pp.* 419, 420.

In the long war that succeeded, Austria bore the heaviest part. Her allies, one by one, left her to meet the power of the French arms led by Bonaparte. Her Italian possessions were snatched from her grasp, her generals beaten, her armies scattered, and, in 1797, she was driven to conclude the Peace of Campo Formio.—*Kohlrausch, pp.* 421–424.

The Second Coalition drew Austria again into a contest with her gigantic foe, and again the empire bore the brunt of

1798. Napoleon's attacks. These repeated strokes soon broke to pieces the ancient and loosely bound fabric of the old German Empire. The century closed upon Austria while she was still reeling under the terrible blows dealt against her at the battles of Marengo and Hohenlinden.—*Allison's Europe, Vol.* 2, *pp.* 104–106, *and pp.* 120, 121.

PRUSSIA.

GERMAN history divided at the opening of the Eighteenth Century. The old empire, much weakened in its bonds, still followed Austria; but another great power had arisen in its midst. Frederick William, the great Elector of Brandenburg, and the real founder of the Prussian monarchy, had, by his wisdom and energy, largely increased the power and extent of his hereditary dominions, which consisted of Brandenburg and the duchy of Prussia, and, in 1688, left to his son Frederick an ample territory, with great wealth.

By permission of the emperor, Leopold I., who desired to secure his aid in the coming war of the Spanish Succes-
1701. sion, Frederick assumed the title of Frederick I., king of Prussia.—*Frederick, I. in Am. Cy. Kohlrausch, p.* 363.

Frederick I. died, February 25th, and left his kingdom, much impoverished by his extravagance, to his son, Frederick
1713. William I., a man of rough temper and boorish manners. By the practice of the closest economy, he recovered his kingdom from debt, and collected a large and efficient army. His passions for tall soldiers and strong beer were the only ones he indulged to excess.—*Frederick William I. in Am. Cy.*

On the 21st of May, Frederick William I. died, and was succeeded on the throne by his son, Frederick II. the Great,
1740. one of the ablest rulers and generals of this century. He was a man of remarkable genius, of liberal learning, and a patron of arts and sciences. His ability and courage, more than once, saved his country from ruin, and laid the broad foundation of its after greatness. He was scarcely seated on his throne, when he plunged into the war of the Austrian Succession, and won Silesia to his crown. His career in the War of Succession and in the Seven Years' War has already been given under "Germany."—*Frederick II. in Am. Cy.*

Frederick II. died, August 17th, after a long reign of unsur-
1786. passed brilliancy, and was succeeded by his nephew,
Frederick William II.

On the death of Frederick William II., he was succeeded by
his son Frederick William III., whose long, eventful,
1797. and prosperous reign did not close till 1840. Frederick took part in the struggles of Europe against Napoleon, and his kingdom suffered some of the consequences of that extraordinary period of great wars. The history of Prussia has been sufficiently traced under the head of "Germany."—*Frederick William III. in Am. Cy. Prussia in Am. Cy.*

HOLLAND AND BELGIUM

HOLLAND, at the opening of the Eighteenth Century, was closely united in sympathy and policy with England through their common sovereign, William III., Stadtholder of Holland and king of England. After his death, in 1702, Holland still continued to co-operate with England in the great struggle, begun by William, against Louis XIV.

The Anti-Orange party being in power, no Stadtholder was chosen to succeed William III, till 1741, when William IV. was made Stadtholder. On his death, in 1751, he was succeeded by his infant son, William V.

The ten provinces known as the Spanish, and afterwards the Austrian, Netherlands, now the kingdom of Belgium, were often the battle field of the great wars of the century, and not unfrequently the prize of the victors.

Holland was always the victim of party strifes of extraordinary bitterness and violence. Towards the close of the century, these parties were the French or democratic party, and the aristocratic party. The Orangists were a third party, smaller, usually, than the others, and sometimes merged with the aristocratic party.

The democratic party getting the ascendancy, deprived William V., the Stadtholder, of his authority, and virtually drove
1786. him into exile.—*Pict. Eng., Vol.* 5, *p.* 653.

Frederick William II. of Prussia, whose sister was the wife of the Stadtholder, interfered, and, marching a Prussian
1787. army into Holland, restored the exile to power.—*Fred., William II. in Am. Cy. Pict. Eng., Vol.* 5, *pp.* 678–682.

The French Revolutionary army under Pichegru advancing into the Netherlands, was welcomed by the Dutch de-
1795. mocrats, and the country, being soon conquered, was erected into the Batavian Republic.—*Netherlands in Am. Cy. Thiers' French Rev., Vol.* 3, *pp.* 182–185.

ITALY.

The Italian States played a subordinate, but still a conspicuous part in the movements of the Eighteenth Century. At the close of the war of the Spanish Succession, Sardinia and Naples fell into the hands of Austria. The Medici family became extinct in 1737, and Francis of Lorraine, the husband of Maria Theresa, became grand duke of Tuscany. The Spanish Bourbon prince, Don Philip, conquered Parma and Piacenza, and was confirmed as hereditary duke of Parma at the Peace of Aix la Chapelle. Thus, a large part of Italy lost its independence, and fell under the control of foreigners.—*Italy in Am. Cy.*

The kingdom of Sardinia grew out of the arrangements made by the treaty of Utrecht and the Quadruple Alliance. In 1720, Victor Amadeus II. was compelled to exchange Sicily, which he had obtained at the Peace of Utrecht, for Sardinia, and henceforward he assumed the title of king of Sardinia.

Victor Amadeus resigned in favor of his brother, Charles Emanuel III. This skillful ruler took advantage of the
1730. contests which raged in Europe to increase his territories. He was succeeded, in 1773, by his son Victor Amadeus III.,

who reigned till 1796, and was succeeded by Charles Emanuel IV.—*Sardinian States in Am. Cy.*

The French army under Napoleon burst upon Northern Italy,
and soon snatched it from Austria and the other powers
1796. which held it. See "France."

Bonaparte erected Milan, Mantua, a portion of Parma, and
Modena into the Cisalpine Republic; Genoa into the
1797. Ligurian Republic; and the Papal States into the Roman
Republic. These republics were not of long duration.—*Italy in Am. Cy.*

NORTHERN AND EASTERN EUROPE.

Northern and Eastern Europe was all aflame with the great wars of the young Swedish hero, Charles XII. when the Eighteenth Century began its course. Charles, having defeated the Russians at Narva, fell like a thunderbolt on Poland, defeated Augustus II., made Stanislaus I. king in his stead, pursued Augustus into Saxony, and spent several years in petty struggles in Saxony and Poland.—*Charles XII. in Am. Cy. Mod. Europe, Vol.* 2, *pp.* 306, 307.

In the meantime, Charles' great rival, Peter the Great, was
busy repairing his losses, and preparing for the future.
1703. Wishing a seaport on the Baltic, he obtained possession
of the river Neva, and among the marshes of its mouth he laid the foundation of St. Petersburg, his future capital.—*Peter I. in Am. Cy.*

In the battle of Pultusk, Charles conquered the Saxons, and drove Augustus of Saxony from the throne of Poland.

Charles, having invaded Russia for the purpose of driving
Peter from his throne, with fool hardy valor, pushed for-
1707. ward into the immense wilds of the Ukraine, and lost
thousands of his army, and most of his artillery and baggage.—*Charles XII. in Am. Cy. Mod. Europe, Vol.* 2, *p.* 337.

Peter, having gathered an army of 70,000 men, fell upon

Charles before Pultowa, July 8th, and, in a bloody battle,
1709. nearly annihilated the Swedish army. Charles himself escaped, with 300 men, into Turkey, where he remained for five years, vainly attempting to incite the Turks to a war against Russia.—*Mod. Europe, Vol.* 2, *pp.* 338–340.

The Turks again marched up the Danube to invade Hungary. Eugene of Savoy was sent against them with an Austrian
1716. army, and defeated them in the great battle of Carlowitz. August 5th. The Turks fled, leaving 30,000 dead on the field, and 250 pieces of artillery were abandoned.—*Abbott's Austria, p.* 360.

Eugene immediately invested Belgrade, which had so often witnessed the assaults of Christians and Turks. He
1717. finally captured it, nearly destroying the Turkish army, and compelling them to another peace.—*Abbott's Austria, p.* 363.

Charles, having been driven out of Turkey, escaped in disguise to Sweden, and renewed the contest against the
1718. foes of his country. But his wild wars had exhausted his unfortunate kingdom. Sweden's glory had passed away, As he was conducting the siege of Frederickshall, he was instantly killed by a grape shot.—*Mod. Eu., Vol.* 2, *pp.* 384–389.

At the Peace of Nystadt, Sweden ceded large territories on the eastern shore of the Baltic to Russia, and Peter sur-
1721. rendered Finland, and paid $2,000,000 in return. This gave Russia a seaboard, and brought it into more immediate communication with western Europe; while, by his wonderful reforms, Peter changed the character of his people, and introduced among them the civilization of the west.—*Peter I. and Russia in Am. Cy.*

February 8th, Peter I. died, and was succeeded by his wife, Catherine I., a woman of coarse but strong mind, whom
1725. Peter had raised from a low, and even infamous, position to become his wife and successor. She ruled with much vigor. —*Catherine in Am. Cy.*

On the death of Catherine I., she was succeeded by Peter II., a grandson of Peter the Great, and now only eleven
1727. years of age. He died in 1730, and was followed by

Anna, a niece of Peter the Great. Under this reign, Siberia was united to Russia.—*Russia in Am. Cy. Abbott's Russia, pp.* 365–367.

Anna, who ruled with great spirit, provoked by some ravages of the Turks and Tartars, attacked them, and, in two
1736. campaigns, over-ran Tartary with fire and sword, and took Asoph and Crimea. Austria was induced to attack the Turks also, but they turned their forces towards their old battle fields in Hungary, and, after winning several advantages, and besieging Belgrade, compelled, in 1737, a peace, in which Belgrade was again surrendered to them.—*Mod. Europe, Vol.* 2, *pp.* 402, 403.

Anna was succeeded, in 1740, by Ivan VII., a mere child, who was dethroned, in 1741, by Elizabeth Petrovna, a daughter of Peter the Great and Catherine I., and a woman of the most infamous character and habits. She, however, reigned with considerable vigor, and favored the introduction of arts and learning. —*Abbott's Russia, pp.* 368–377.

Elizabeth died after a reign of twenty years, and was succeeded by her nephew, Peter III., a brute in human form.
1762. Elizabeth had been in alliance with Maria Theresa, and had sent a Russian army to assist her in the Seven Years' War. The drunken and imbecile Peter was a great admirer of Frederick the Great, and on coming to the throne, he immediately forbade his armies to co-operate with the Austrians, and soon after ordered them to obey the commands of Frederick. This timely change saved Frederick and Prussia.—*Abbott's Russia, p.* 377.

Catherine, the wife of the brutal Peter, July 19th, raised an insurrection against her husband, and assumed the crown as Catherine II. She reigned with great sagacity and brilliancy.—*Abbott's Russia, pp.* 391–393.

Another of those terrible Turkish wars broke out, and convulsed eastern Europe for six years. The Turks,
1768. alarmed at the prospect of the further aggrandizement of Russia by the absorption of Poland, declared war, and sent 250-000 men into the field. The Greeks took advantage of the war

to make an insurrection, which was suppressed with the most awful severity.—*Mod. Europe, Vol.* 3, *pp.* 49–55.

The successors of Charles XII. ruled with restricted authority. The nobles having extorted a Constitution giving them-
1771. selves large powers, the government was really an Aristocracy. Sweden was compelled to make large cessions of its territories, and it recovered very slowly from the ruinous wars of its hero king.

Adolphus Frederick, after a turbulent reign of twenty years, died in 1771, and was succeeded by his son, Gustavus III. There were two parties in the State at this time, the "Hats," or the party of "France and Commerce," and the "Caps," or the party of "Russia and Agriculture." Gustavus, taking advantage of the prevalent strifes, by a bold but bloodless blow, accomplished, in 1772, a revolution which restored the monarchal Constitution. He waged a successful war against Russia from 1787 to 1790. After a turbulent reign, he was assassinated in 1792, and was succeeded by his son. Gustavus IV.—*Gustavus III. in Am. Cy. Mod. Eu., Vol.* 3, *pp.* 55–57.

Poland having been long torn with domestic convulsions and civil wars, Russia, Prussia, and Austria took advantage
1772. of this condition of affairs to partition among them a large portion of its territories.—*Mod. Eu., Vol.* 3, *pp.* 43–49.

Again the Turks resorted to arms to resist the threatening growth of Russian power, and for nearly five years, blood
1787. flowed like water under the blows of the terrible Suwarroff.—*Suwarroff and Catherine II. in Am. Cy.*

A second partition of Polish territories, made in 1793, drove the desparing nation into insurrection, under the lead of
1794. the great Polish chieftain, Kosciusko. But Poland was not equal to the task, and Kosciusko was finally defeated in the bloody battle of Maciejovice, and with him fell Polish independence.—*Kosciusko and Poland in Am. Cy.*

Russia, Prussia, and Austria now proceeded to divide the last fragment of the ancient and once powerful kingdom of
1795. Poland between them, and it disappeared finally from the map of nations.—*Poland in Am. Cy.*

After a long and prosperous reign, Catherine died, November
1796. 17th, and was succeeded by her son, Paul I., an ignorant
barbarian despot. Russia, now grown to an overshadowing greatness, began to mingle her voice in the affairs of western Europe. Paul joined the Coalition against France, and 100,000 Russians marched to swell the allied armies. Russian blood flowed in torrents on the battle fields of Italy. Paul soon withdrew from the Coalition, and made peace with Napoleon.—*Abbott's Russia, pp.* 464–467.

The Eighteenth Century went out amidst a whirlwind. A genius of gigantic power had appeared upon the scene, and Europe stood aghast at his success. The beaten nations held their breath to see what would come next from this prodigy, and the curtain fell.

GENERAL VIEW

OF THE

NINETEENTH CENTURY.

IF there is any one word which can fitly portray the Nineteenth Century that word is PROGRESS. It is peculiarly the age of progress. Other centuries have exhibited gigantic movements and agitations, but these movements have been chiefly conflicts or revolutions. The movements of this century have been marches; its agitations, advances. History, in all periods, shows to the careful observer some slow but certain progression; but the progress of the Nineteenth Century has been so swift and splendid, that all eyes have been attracted by it. It is a theme of daily remark among all classes, and, shaping itself into a popular creed, it has become the battle-cry of the age. It is as if the long pent energies of mankind, boiling and raging often in revolts and revolutions, but always rising, under whatever mountain weights of oppression, had at length broken all barriers, and were now flowing forth into the great channels of its destiny.

Political life, after ages of apparently aimless experiments, now seeks to incarnate itself in settled constitutions. Profoundly observing the inalienable rights of man, and the inherent laws of social order and progress, it seeks to embody these more and more fully in its written forms of government, and thus advances to more perfect, as well as more permanent, political organizations. The nations are rapidly marching forward to the point when they shall exhibit not a ruler and a rabble, a privileged few and an oppressed multitude, but great and free peoples, marshalled into true human societies. Not a nation in Christendom but has greatly modified its constitution since the stormy morning hour of this century.

The consolidation of petty and hostile states into great and powerful empires, which forms a distinguishing feature of the century, is both a proof and a cause of its political progress. Fraternization is one of the mightiest agencies, as it is also one of the most beneficent ends of human civilization. Humanity, not mere nationality, is the last word of history. Philanthropy is nobler as well as broader than patriotism.

The number of separate governments in Europe has greatly diminished since the opening of this century. Even some old though small nationalities have been compelled to yield to this prevalent tendency of the age. Poland, Hungary, and Ireland have succumbed to the inevitable fiat. A united Italy, a consolidated Germany, and a preserved union of the American States, if not a grander Britain, and a mightier Russia, may yet be found to compensate for the disappearance of some of the minor tribal divisions from the map of the world.

But the political progress of the century has not been an unbroken advance. It has rather been a succession of wave-like movements, followed by apparent recessions. The first great wave broke, in 1815, on the battle-field of Waterloo, and was succeeded by reactionary efforts of the Holy Alliance. The second culminated in the revolutions and reform movements of 1830, and were followed by the comparative quiet and apathy of the next few years. The third wave broke in the great revolutions of '48, and was succeeded by the reactions of '50. Later movements are too near, and too incomplete to be wisely judged.

The most striking characteristic of the political history of "the Great Century," is the new position occupied by the People in public affairs. From being the mere *subjects* of government, they have become virtual *sovereigns*. Formerly, there were no people in politics; now, there is nothing but the people. The Eighteenth Century emancipated the people; the Nineteenth has empowered them. The Eighteenth Century vindicated their rights; the Nineteenth is vindicating their authority. The highest political utterance of the Eighteenth Century was that governments are instituted "to secure the rights" of men, and "derive their powers from the consent of the governed." The highest political utterance of the Nineteenth, made by the martyr President, is "the government of the People, by the People, for the People." Europe, resisting these doctrines of popular sovereignty has met the stormy crises of popular revolt; and her governments present the aspect of retreat before the advancing power of the people. America accepts these doctrines, and its government and people advance together.

But the grandest features of the Nineteenth Century are not political, nor governmental. Governments are means, not ends, in a people's life. The People's Century is a century of trade and thought—of arts and science—of steam-ships and Crystal Palaces, and Atlantic Telegraphs. It may be safely affirmed that no former age of history ever exhibited such progress in the arts as this. Mankind stand amazed at their own triumphs, and question whether they have not nearly reached the limits of possible progress. Commerce has arisen from the menial employment of a few private citizens to the rank of a great and over-shadowing interest of the State, compelling governments to make peace or war as it shall dictate. Its princes are more powerful than crowned kings. Mechanic art has doubled, many times over, the working and wealth-producing power of the race, and the wildest legends of magic have been more than equalled by the inventions of this age. The steam-ship, the railroad, the telegraph, the power press, the photograph, the vulcanized rubber, the mowers and reapers, the sewing and knitting machines, the needle gun and the iron-clad monitor, are mightier slaves for man's service than all the genii summoned by Aladdin's lamp. And science has kept pace with art. It has left no realm unexplored, and has explored no field in vain. It has doubled the volume of human knowledge, and has replaced, with well established truths, much of the mere conjectures of earlier times. It is too soon to estimate the literature of the century, but we may well believe that it has added many a grand book, which the world will not willingly let die.

But the crowning glory of the age is its great national systems of public instruction. The free school is the noblest compliment the human mind ever paid to its own essential worth and greatness. It vindicates the rights of the intellect, and must react with a tremendous and cumulative power upon the progress and civilization of the race.

Nor would the picture of the century be complete without some notice of its religious movements. Never was Christianity so active, and never were its triumphs so great, and its conquests so rapid. Waking to the grand import of its divine founder's last command, it has armed itself in earnest for the conquest of the world. It is the age of missions. Preachers are treading every heathen shore, and penetrating every barbarian wild. The Bible has been translated into hundreds of languages, and its copies multiplied to many millions. Its great doctrines have been more profoundly examined, and more strongly established, and its benign power is more widely felt than ever before since its last page was written.

Such are some of the main features of the century which Victor Hugo has justly called "the Great Century," and whose history exhibits more triumphs, and presents more problems, than any other in the long roll of time. Its sunset promises to be as glorious as its morning was stormy and dark.

AMERICA.

THE United States entered the Nineteenth Century under the presidency of John Adams, with sixteen States, and a population of 5,305,937 souls. The storm raging in Europe had agitated the sea of American politics. The Federalists, who supported President Adams, favored England. The Republicans favored France, and succeeded, in the autumn of 1800, in electing their candidate to the presidency. The farewell address of the beloved Washington had given timely warning to his countrymen against being entangled in foreign alliances, and the country outrode, in peace, the storm that swept Europe. The century, in American history, has been one of unexampled growth. No where has the spirit of progress exhibited its power on so grand a scale. The world never before saw a history so marked with the sudden and gigantic growth of a great empire by peaceful agencies. Free government has vindicated itself forever in the power and prosperity of our country.

Jefferson was inaugurated on the 4th of March. Aaron Burr
1801. was Vice-President, and James Madison, Secretary of
State.—*Lossing, p.* 388.

Ohio, a part of the original Northwestern Territory, was ad-
1802. mitted to the Union.—*United States in Am. Cy. Lossing, p.* 390.

The United States purchased the Territory of Louisiana from
1803. the French government for $15,000,000, the French
having acquired it a few years before, by secret treaty, from Spain. Out of this were formed the Territory of New Orleans and the District of Louisiana.—*Lossing, p.* 390.

On the 12th of July, the Vice-President, Aaron Burr, chal-
1804. lenged Alexander Hamilton to a duel, and brutally shot
him. This duel, which grew out of political strifes, may serve to show the rancor of party spirit in those days.—*Lossing, p.* 396. *A. Hamilton in Am. Cy.*

The Algerine corsairs having committed great depredations on American ships, a war broke out between the two countries in 1801. In 1804, Tripoli was bombarded by the American fleet, under Commodore Preble, and an invasion of its territories was made, in 1805, by Captain William Eaton. Peace was restored in 1805.—*Lossing, pp.* 390–395. *U. S. in Am. Cy.*

Jefferson was re-elected this year with but little opposition.—*Lossing, p.* 396.

Aaron Burr's conspiracy for establishing an independent gov-
1806. ernment in the southwest belonged principally to this
year, though begun in 1805.—*Lossing, pp.* 396–398. *Burr in Am. Cy.*

The retaliating measures of France and England bearing
1807. ruinously on American commerce, an Embargo Act was
passed by Congress, confining all vessels at home, and cutting off all commerce with France and England. This Em-

bargo produced great distress, and threatened to disrupt the Union.—*Lossing, pp.* 400, 403.

Robert Fulton this year made the first successful attempt at steam navigation, his steamboat, the "Clermont," making several trips between New York and Albany. Many successful experiments of propelling boats by steam power had been made before, both in Great Britain and in the United States.—*Steam Navigation in Am. Cy.*

The Constitution permitting an abolition of the infamous slave-trade this year, Congress passed an act abolishing
1808. the importation of slaves.—*Slavery in Am. Cy.*

Jefferson having declined a re-election, the Republicans, now beginning to be called Democrats, nominated and
1809. elected James Madison, who was inaugurated March 4th. The country was full of animosity and gloom. Commerce was prostrated by the Embargo, and war threatened with England, France, and Spain.—*Lossing, p.* 404. *U. S. in Am. Cy.*

The South American Provinces had remained mostly in the colonial state, and under the control of Spain. Brazil
1810. belonged to Portugal, and Guiana to the Dutch and French. The sound of the great European storm reached even to these remote colonies, and stirred the spirit of revolt. Ecquador revolted in 1809, and Venezuela in 1810. In 1810, New Grenada declared independence, which was not fully secured till 1819.—*Venezuela, Ecquador, New Grenada, and Bolivar in Am. Cy.*

Venezuela now declared independence, and finally obtained it as a member of the Republic of Columbia, proclaimed
1811. by Bolivar in 1819.—*Bolivar and Columbia in Am. Cy.*

This year, an Indian war broke out, under the lead of Tecumseh, a Shawnee chief. The Indians attacked General Harrison at Tippecanoe, but were repulsed after a severe battle.—*Lossing, p.* 408.

The difficulties with England at last compelled the United States to declare war, June 19th. The Federalists
1812. strongly opposed this war, and organized the Peace Party.

General Hull, governor of Michigan, attempted an invasion

of Canada from Detroit, but, August 16th, surrendered Detroit, with all his army and stores, to the British General Brock.—*Lossing, p.* 411.

October 13th, a force crossed over to Canada and captured Queenstown Heights. In the afternoon, a fresh force of British and Indians came up and recaptured the Heights, taking or killing the entire American force.—*Lossing, pp.* 413, 414.

The British government declared the whole coast under blockade, except that of New England, hoping to detach the New England States from the Union.

On the 19th of August, the United States frigate Constitution met the British frigate Guerriere near the American coast, and, after a contest of forty minutes, the Guerriere surrendered, a complete wreck.

On the 18th of October, the sloop Wasp captured the British brig Frolic; October 25th, the frigate United States fought and captured the British frigate Macedonian; December 29th, the Constitution met and conquered the British ship Java in a bloody battle.—*Lossing, p.* 415.

These splendid naval victories compensated for the defeats on land, and filled the Americans with pride.

Beside the several victories gained by the regular navy, the American privateers were also successful in many encounters. It was estimated that in 1812, more than fifty armed vessels and two hundred and fifty merchantmen were captured by the Americans. At this time, the British navy numbered 1060 vessels, that of the United States, exclusive of gun-boats, numbered only 20.—*Lossing, p.* 414.

Madison entered on his second term. The country was now thoroughly roused, and the campaign opened early.

1813. General Harrison assembled an army of the West, near the western end of Lake Erie; General Dearborn, an army of the Center, at Niagara; and General Hampton, the army of the North, near Lake Champlain. January 22d, a battle was fought on the Raisin, near Monroe, Michigan. The American force of nearly 1,300 men, under General Winchester, was surprised and defeated, and the next day the Indians massacred all the sick and wounded. May 1st, General Harrison was besieged in Fort Meigs by a large force of British and Indians, who were finally compelled to abandon the siege. A later attempt in August also failed.—*Lossing, pp.* 416–420.

September 10th, a naval battle was fought near the western end of Lake Erie, and a decisive victory gained by the Americans, under Commodore Perry.—*Lossing, p.* 420.

Harrison immediately crossed to attack Malden, but found that Proctor and Tecumseh had fled to the Thames, abandoning both Malden and Detroit. Harrison pursued, and, October 5th, totally defeated the British and Indians in the battle of the Thames, Tecumseh being among the killed.—*Los., pp.* 423, 424.

Several other battles were fought with various success near Lake Ontario and Lake George. The Americans captured Toronto, then York, and the British captured and burned several villages, Buffalo being of the number.—*Lossing, pp.* 425–427.

Tecumseh, early in the spring, had visited the southern tribes of Indians, and roused them to hostilities. A furious Indian war broke out, and terrible massacres were effected, till General Jackson was sent against them, and utterly defeated them in several bloody battles.—*Lossing, pp.* 427, 428.

Numerous naval battles were fought during the year, the balance of the victories being in favor of the Americans, though they lost the Chesapeake in a short but severe engagement with the British frigate Shannon.—*Lossing, pp.* 428–430.

The defeat of Napoleon, early this year, enabled England to send a large force to America. The war raged along

1814. the Canada line. The British defeated General Wilkinson near the north end of Lake Champlain, March 30th, and captured Oswego, May 6th. But, July 5th, the Americans gained the victory of Chippewa, and, on the 25th, they fought and won the severe battle of Lundy's Lane, near Niagara Falls. —*Lossing, pp.* 432, 433.

In August, a heavy British force was sent to Chesapeake Bay, and, on the 24th, after defeating a militia force, entered Washington, and burned the public buildings. They then advanced on Baltimore, fighting and repulsing another militia force; but they were finally foiled in their purpose, and silently withdrew, after bombarding fort McHenry. The whole Atlantic coast was annoyed by marauding parties landing from British vessels.—*—Lossing, pp.* 436, 437.

September 11, Commodore MacDonough fought the naval battle of Plattsburgh on Lake Champlain, and completely defeated the British forces.—*Lossing, p.* 435.

Negotiations for peace were begun in 1813, but the Peace of Ghent was not signed till December 24th, 1814.—*Los., p.* 444.

Before the news of the peace reached America, a British force
invaded Louisiana, and were defeated in the Battle of
1815. New Orleans. fought January 8th, in which Jackson
gained one of the most brilliant victories of the war.—*Lossing, pp.* 439, 440.

This war cost the United States about $100,000,000, and the loss of lives was estimated at 30,000. The British loss was much greater, both in life and treasure.

The government of Algiers, taking advantage of the war which engaged the American forces and fleets, began again its depredations on American commerce. Commodore Decatur proceeded to the Mediterranean, gained some victories, and compelled the Algerines to set at liberty the American captives and make peace.—*Lossing, p.* 445.

The United States bank was incorporated with a capital of
$35,000,000, and with a charter to run twenty years.
1816. In December, Indiana was admitted into the Union.—
Lossing, p. 446.

March 4th, James Monroe, of Virginia, having been elected
by the Democratic party, which had then a very large
1817. majority, was inaugurated President, and Daniel D.
Tompkins, of New York, Vice-President. The Federalists, who had bitterly opposed the war to the end, were almost extinguished as a party. Democrats and Federalists united to support the administration.—*United States in Am. Cy.*

December 10th, the State of Mississippi was admitted to the Union. Another Indian war broke out in the south, instigated by British emissaries.—*Lossing, p.* 448.

December 3d, Illinois was admitted, increasing the number of
1818. States to twenty-one. Populations were now pouring into the great American wilderness, and State after State emerged into the field of historic life—*Illinois in Am. Cy.*

December 14th, Alabama was admitted. The jealousies
1819. between the slaveholding and free States were already at work, and the admission of each free State was offset by the admission of a slave State. The admission of Alabama destroyed the balance and awakened agitation.—*U.S. in Am. Cy.*

This year, Florida was ceded by Spain to the United States. —*Florida in Am. Cy.*

The revolts of the South American provinces, under the lead of their wretched and incompetent chiefs, had dragged slowly through nine years. Simon Bolivar, a miserable boaster, without courage or capacity, had repeatedly ruined the cause, which had been repeatedly restored by abler men and by foreign aid. He was finally induced, by advice of some foreigners, to proclaim the "Republic of Columbia," embracing New Granada and Venezuela. After a miserable existence of twelve years, rent by intestine divisions, it was dissolved, in 1831, into the three independent republics of New Granada, Venezuela, and Ecquador. —*Bolivar and Columbia in Am. Cy.*

Maine and Missouri both applied for admission into the
1820. Union, the former as a free State, the latter as a slave State. Maine was admitted in March; but a determined opposition was made to the admission of Missouri. A strong anti-slavery feeling had arisen in the north in all parties, aroused by the steady extension of slavery, and, in 1818–19, an attempt was made in Congress to prescribe an Anti-Slavery Constitution for Missouri. Congress and the entire country were filled with violent agitations.

The storm was finally allayed by the adoption, February 28th,
1821. of the so-called Missouri Compromise, prohibiting slavery forever in the territories north of the line of 36 degrees 30 minutes north latitude. Missouri was admitted by the same act.—Monroe entered upon his second term, there having been but one vote against him.—*United States in Am. Cy.*

July 28th, Peru was declared independent, and General San Martin, who had invaded the country with an army of Chilians, was proclaimed Protector.—*Peru in Am. Cy.*

This year, Guatemala also declared independence.—*Guatemala in Am. Cy.*

The United States, under the eloquent appeals of Henry Clay, acknowledged the independence of the South American
1822. Republics *(Mallory's Life and Speeches of Clay)*, and Monroe, in his next annual message, announced the "Monroe Doctrine," that the American Continents are, henceforth, not to be considered as subjects for future colonization by any European power.—*United States in Am. Cy.*

The Brazilians, provoked by the oppressive acts of Portugal, under whose control they were, proclaimed independence, and established the Empire of Brazil, conferring the imperial crown on Don Pedro, son of John VI. of Portugal, under the title of Pedro I.—*Brazil in Am. Cy.*

Mexico had revolted and declared independence of Spain in 1810, but the revolt, after several years, was suppressed.
1823. In 1821, a second revolution was undertaken to establish an independent monarchy, and Iturbide, its leader, became Emperor. An insurrection, under Santa Anna, compelled Iturbide to abdicate, March 20th, 1823, and Mexico became a republic with nineteen states and four territories.—*Mexico in Am. Cy.*

La Fayette revisited the country he had helped to free, and the nation resounded with welcomes and rejoicing wher-
1824. ever he appeared.—*Lossing, p.* 453.

Mainly by the efforts of Henry Clay, a Protective Tariff Bill was passed, April 16th. Thus was inaugurated the "American System," the subject, at a later day, of such bitter party strifes. —*Mallory's Life and Speeches of Henry Clay, Vol.* 1, *pp.* 110, 111.

The number of candidates voted for, prevented any election of President by the people, and John Quincy Adams was
1825. elected by the House of Representatives from the several names presented by the electors. In politics, he agreed with Monroe. He was inaugurated March 4th.—*Lossing, p.* 454.

The gigantic work of internal improvement, the Erie Canal,

was completed, and opened this year with great celebrations.—*De Witt Clinton in Am. Cy.*

The first railroad in the United States was completed this
1827. year from the granite quarries of Quincy, Massachusetts,
to Neponset river. It was worked by horse power.
Railroads had been constructed in France and England a year or two earlier. They were rapidly extended to all parts of the country, and, in 1861, amounted, in the United States, to 48,100 miles, costing $1,177,994,428.00.—*Railroad in Am. Cy.*

Bolivar, by the aid of the army, was raised to the post of Dic-
1828. tator of the Republic of Columbia.—*Bolivar in Am. Cy.*
Uruguay was erected into the Republic of Oriental Uruguay. It is more nearly a military despotism.—*Uruguay in Am. Cy.*

This year, a new Tariff law was passed, to protect American manufacturers, but it met with bitter opposition from the southern states.—*United States in Am. Cy. Lossing, p.* 459.

Andrew Jackson was inaugurated as President, and John C.
1829. Calhoun as Vice-President. Party spirit was again running high, and the iron will of Jackson added to the strife.

The Bank Controversy, concerning the renewal of the charter
1832. of the United States Bank, arrayed the country in two parties—Bank men and Anti-Bank men. The Bank men took the name of Whigs. The Bank party triumphed in Congress, and passed a bill for renewing the charter. Jackson vetoed it as unconstitutional.—*United States in Am. Cy.*

The southern states opposed the tariff, and, at length, the opposition grew so bold, that South Carolina declared the law null; and, having armed to resist the collection of duties, threatened to secede if it should be enforced by military power. Jackson met the crisis with great promptness, threatening to hang John C. Calhoun. The "nullifiers" quailed and submitted. The debates in Congress during this contest were remarkable for eloquence. Webster's great speech against nullification and secession, in 1830, is of marvelous power. The conflict was ended by the Compromise of 1833.—*U. S. in Am. Cy. Lossing, p.* 464.

The Sac Indians, under the lead of their chief, Black Hawk, made war against the whites in Wisconsin and Illinois. He was finally captured, and the Indians driven across the Mississippi. —*Lossing p.* 463.

Jackson, led by his strong hatred of the United States Bank,
1833. recommended the removal of the public funds from its
care, and Congress refusing, he took the responsibility, after the adjournment, and ordered them to be removed. Immense excitement followed this act.—*United States in Am. Cy.*

The anti-slavery agitation again arose. The American Anti-Slavery Society was formed, and began the issue of pamphlets and periodicals to enlighten the public mind. The southern leaders also began to denounce and resist the anti-slavery sentiment as a means of uniting and "firing" the southern people.—*Slavery in Am. Cy. Benton's Thirty Years' View, Vol.* 1, *Chap.* 135.

Congress having directed the removal of the Seminole Indians
1835. from Florida, the Indians took up arms, under their chief,
Osceola, and a cruel war succeeded. After many battles and much bloodshed, the savages were conquered.—*Lossing, pp.* 466–468.

The anti-slavery agitation was greatly increased this year by the attempt of Calhoun and other southern men to secure an act of Congress prohibiting the circulation of anti-slavery papers through the mails.—*Benton's Thirty Years' View, Vol.* 1, *Chap.* 131. *United States in Am. Cy, p.* 768.

Arkansas was admitted to the Union as a slave State, and, in
1836. 1837, Michigan came in as a free State.—*Arkansas and
Michigan in Am. Cy.*

Martin Van Buren, having been elected by the Democratic
1837. party to the Presidency, was inaugurated, March 4th.
Richard M. Johnson was chosen Vice-President by the Senate, the people having failed to make an election. Van Buren pursued the policy inaugurated by Jackson.

A great financial revulsion occurred this year, and bankruptcy and distress abounded. The independent treasury system was proposed by the President as a remedy for the disorders, and "*the Sub-Treasury Scheme*," as it was called, became the great political question of the day.—*Lossing, pp.* 470, 471.

The Canada Rebellion, under McKenzie and Papineau, occurred this year, and threatened to involve the United States in a war with England.

The United States exploring expedition to the South Seas was sent out under the command of Commodore Wilkes. The cruise occupied four years. The discovery of the Antarctic Continent was made by this expedition.—*Wilkes in Am. Cy.*

In the elections held in 1840, the Whigs were successful, and General William H. Harrison, their candidate, became
1841. President. A month after his inauguration, he died, and John Tyler, the Vice-President, became President. Tyler's vetoes of the charters passed for a new national bank, separated him from his party, though Webster, the great Whig statesman, still remained Secretary of State.—*United States in Am. Cy.*

The boundary between Maine and New Brunswick had never been clearly defined. Disputes at length arose among
1842. the border settlers, and both governments sent troops into the disputed territory to protest their rights. War seemed imminent between England and the United States, but a treaty, negotiated by Webster and Lord Ashburton, at length, settled the question, which, in a more barbarous age, would certainly have led to a bloody conflict.—*Webster in Am. Cy.*

Texas revolted from Mexico, of which it formed a part, and, in 1836, declared independence. Its annexation to the
1845. United States was effected under Tyler's administration, March 1st, 1845. It had been urged by southern statesmen to increase the area of slavery, and caused violent agitations throughout the whole country. It was the great issue in the excited elections of 1844.—*United States in Am. Cy. Benton's Thirty Year's View, Vol.* 2, *Chaps.* 135 *and* 148.

Two days later, Tyler signed the bill admitting Florida and Iowa into the Union.—*United States in Am. Cy.*

March 4th, James K. Polk was inaugurated as President, and George M. Dallas as Vice-President.—*Lossing, p.* 478.

It had been charged by the opponents of the admission of

Texas, that its admission would lead to war with Mexico,
1846. that country not having yet acknowledged the independence of its revolted provinces. The war, as predicted, opened in the spring of 1846. May 8th, the battle of Palo Alto was fought, and the victory gained by the United States troops under General Taylor. The next day they won a second victory at Resaca de la Palma. These victories completely broke up the Mexican army, and sent them back across the Rio Grande. In August, General Taylor crossed the Rio Grande, and captured Matamoras, and, September 24th, captured Monterey, after a siege of four days.—*Lossing, pp.* 481–484.

John C. Fremont led a party over the mountains to California, and, defeating a Mexican force, proclaimed California independent.

It being foreseen that we should gain a considerable increase of territory by this war, David Wilmot proposed in Congress the "Wilmot Proviso," that no slavery should exist in such territory. This greatly increased the anti-slavery agitation in the country.—*United States in Am. Cy.*

February 22d, General Taylor, whose army had been greatly
reduced by forces sent to General Scott, was surrounded,
1847. at Buena Vista, by a large Mexican army under Santa Anna. The next day, a long and bloody battle was fought, and the Mexicans were defeated.—*Lossing, p.* 486.

In March, General Scott besieged and captured Vera Cruz. He then marched to the city of Mexico, winning, on his way, several brilliant and important victories, and finally taking the capital after several days of severe fighting.—*Los., pp.* 489–494.

General Kearney, who had been sent with another army to conquer New Mexico and California, found his work in California done, and proclaimed its anexation to the United States. —*Lossing, p.* 487.

In February, a treaty of peace was concluded with Mexico,
the United States giving Mexico $12,000,000 for the
1848. territories of California and New Mexico, conquered from her. During the same month, gold was discovered in California, and, soon after, thousands of gold-hunters from all parts of the

world rushed in wild excitement to the scene.—*Lossing, p.* 497. *California in Am. Cy.*

Wisconsin was admitted to the Union, increasing the number of states to thirty.

General Taylor was nominated and elected to the Presidency
by the Whigs in 1848, the *Wilmot Proviso* being one of
1849. the chief issues, and a new Free Soil Party appearing in
the field. March 4th, 1849, President Taylor was inaugurated, Millard Fillmore being Vice-President.

President Taylor died, July 9th, and Fillmore became President
dent in his stead. California, having adopted an Anti-
1850. Slavery Constitution, applied for admission into the
Union. The southern slavery propagandists, enraged at this result of their work, opposed the admission, and threatened disunion. A disunion Southern Convention met at Nashville. Finally, a Compromise was proposed by the aged statesman, Henry Clay, admitting California, and enacting a stringent law for the return of fugitive slaves to their masters, with several other measures. The Compromise measures were adopted, but the excitement in both sections grew more violent. The storm had evidently passed beyond the power of compromises to allay it. A deep-seated desire for disunion was spreading through the South.—*Benton's Thirty Years, Vol.* 2, *Chaps.* 196, 197, *and* 198. *United States in Am. Cy.*

Kossuth, the great Hungarian Chieftain, visited America, and
by his singularly eloquent speeches, aroused a general
1851. sympathy with his cause. This helped to calm, for
some time, the public mind.—*Kossuth in Am. Cy.*

Southern adventurers made an invasion of Cuba, the South being determined, in some way, to compensate for the loss of California.—*United States in Am. Cy. Cuba in Am. Cy.*

Franklin Pierce of New Hampshire, became President, and
William R. King of Alabama, Vice-President. They
1853. were Democrats. Jefferson Davis of Mississippi, became
Secretary of War. The Whig party supported General Scott, and the Free Soil party, John P. Hale.

Senator Douglas introduced into Congress, a bill for the organi-

zation of Kansas and Nebraska territories, in which was
1854. a clause, repealing the *Missouri Compromise*, prohibiting slavery north of 36 deg. 30 min. After a long and stormy debate, the bill passed, May 31st, and the whole country launched afresh into the most violent agitation. Emigrant Aid Societies in New England sent settlers into Kansas to secure it for freedom, and the border men of Missouri resorted to force to keep out, or drive out, these settlers. Armed bands from Missouri took possession of the polls and carried the elections. Murders were common, and civil war raged for several years. After innumerable outrages, the Free State men triumphed.—*Kansas and United States in Am. Cy.*

The Ostend Circular, issued this year by the American ministers to France, Spain, and England, proposed to buy Cuba for $120,000,000, or, if Spain refused to sell, to take it by force to prevent the emancipation of slaves.

William Walker of Tennessee, invaded Nicaraugua with a band of filibusters. He finally got possession of the
1855. country, and being elected President, he revoked the prohibition against slavery. It is believed this was another southern attempt to extend slavery. Walker was finally defeated, captured, and executed in 1857.—*United States in Am. Cy. William Walker in Am. Cy.*

In May, Charles Sumner, having made a powerful but severe speech in the Senate, containing an attack on South
1856. Carolina, was assaulted in the Senate Chamber by Preston S. Brooks of that state, and so injured, that he was obliged to leave Congress. This outrage was applauded by the South, and caused great excitement throughout the country, and added to the animosity between the two sections.—*Sumner in Am. Cy.*

In this excited condition of the country the general election took place. The Republicans, made up of the Free Soil party, most of the Whigs, and some of the Democrats, voted for John C. Fremont, and the Democrats for James Buchanan. The latter was elected. A party known as the "Know Nothings," or American party, supported Millard Fillmore.

Buchanan was inaugurated March 4th, John C. Breckinridge
1857. of Kentucky, being Vice-President. The Kansas troubles still continued.—*U. S. in Am. Cy.*

Minnesota was admitted into the Union. In Kansas a Con-
1858. vention, elected by the "border ruffians", met at Lecompton, 1857, adopted a State Constitution recognizing slavery, and applied to Congress for admission. It was opposed by Douglas and many other Democrats, but finally passed, with a provision submitting it to the people of Kansas, who at once rejected it.—*United States in Am. Cy.*

Oregon was admitted as a state. The mighty wave of popu-
1859. lation had reached the Pacific, and was sweeping up its coasts.

This year, John Brown, an anti-slavery enthusiast, attempted an invasion of Virginia in hopes of provoking a general insurrection and liberation of the slaves. He was taken and hung with several of his followers. This raid created additional excitement, both North and South.—*Greeley's Am. Conflict, Vol.* 1, *pp.* 289–298. *United States in Am. Cy.*

The Democratic National Convention met in Charleston,
1860. South Carolina, in May; but, after violent debates, the southern delegates withdrew, and the Convention adjourned to Baltimore, where the northern delegates nominated, as their candidate for President, Stephen A. Douglas. Most of the southern delegates again seceded, and, holding a separate Convention, nominated J. C. Breckinridge. Another party, calling itself the Constitutional Union Party, nominated John Bell of Tennessee. The Republican Convention met at Chicago, May 16th, and nominated for the Presidency, Abraham Lincoln of Illinois. At the election in November, Lincoln was elected by the vote of the free states.

As soon as Lincoln's election was known, the South Carolina Legislature called a Convention to consider the question of secession. December 17th, the Convention assembled, and, on the 20th, adopted an ordinance declaring the union of South Carolina with the United States dissolved. Thus was the crime, plotted for years, consumated.—*Am. Con., Vol.* 1, *pp.* 332–346.

The last terrible act in the long drama of slavery-agitation was now opened. The state forces, which had long been drilling for the conflict, now siezed the custom house, the post office, and Fort Moultrie, Major Anderson who held it having evacuated it and removed to Fort Sumter.—*Am. Conflict, Vol.* 1, *pp.* 407–410.

The example of South Carolina was rapidly followed by other
1861. states. Mississippi seceded January 9th; Florida, January 10th; Alabama, January 11th; Georgia, January 19th; Louisiana, January 26th; and Texas, February 1st. In all these states the arsenals, custom houses, forts, &c., belonging to the United States, were seized, except Fort Sumter, in South Carolina, and Fort Pickens, in Florida. President Buchanan declared there was no authority to coerce a sovereign state, and Congress occupied itself with compromise measures, to induce a return of the seceded states. February 4th, a Congress of the seceded states was held at Montgomery, a Constitution was adopted, and Jeff. Davis chosen President.

January 28th, Kansas was finally admitted to the Union.

March 4th, Lincoln, after an extended tour from his home in Illinois to Washington, and after escaping assassination only by passing Baltimore in disguise, was inaugurated amidst an immense concourse of people. His inaugural was so full of kindness and wisdom, it might well allay any alarm felt by the southern people.—*Am. Conflict, Vol.* 1, *p.* 422.

April 11th, an attack was made on Fort Sumter, and, on the 13th, it surrendered.—*U. S. in Am. Cy. Am. Conflict, Vol.* 1, *p.* 440.

Thus the war was actually opened, amid insane rejoicings in the South. The silent North awoke as from a troubled sleep. April 15th, President Lincoln's proclamation was flashed over the country for 75,000 volunteers, and, within twenty-four hours, troops began pouring into Washington.—*United States in Am. Cy. Am. Conflict, Vol* 1, *Chap.* 29.

The fall of Sumter hastened the work of secession. Virginia, Arkansas, North Carolina, and Tennessee followed in quick succession, increasing the Southern Confederacy to eleven states.

Missouri and Kentucky decided to remain neutral, and Maryland and Deleware were only saved by the presence of Federal bayonets. United States forts, arsenals, and navy yards were everywhere seized or destroyed, and the South, long prepared for the conflict, thought its work half done. Western Virginia refused to concur in the secession, and established a separate state government.—*Am. Conflict, Vol.* 1, *Chap.* 30.

May 24th, the Union forces advanced into Virginia, and took possession of Alexandria and Arlington Heights. The rebels established themselves at Manassas. In June and July, the Union troops from Ohio and Indiana gained several victories in Western Virginia.—*Am. Conflict, Vol.* 1, *Chap.* 32.

July 21st, the battle of Bull Run was fought, in which the Union forces under General McDowell, after nearly winning a great victory, were seized with a panic, and fled in confusion to Washington.—*Am. Conflict, Vol.* 1, *Chap.* 33.

The next day, General McClellan was placed in chief command, and Congress immediately ordered the calling out of 500-000 men.

August 28th and 29th, Forts Hatteras and Clark, at the entrance to Pamlico Sound, were taken by the Union Commodore Stringham, and, November 7th, Port Royal was taken by an expedition under General T. W. Sherman.

Several battles were fought in Missouri, in one of which General Lyon was killed. July 9th, General Fremont was sent to take command in Missouri, but was superseded, November 2d, by General Hunter. The sad defeat at Ball's Bluff occurred October 21st.—the Union victory of Drainsville, December 20th.

The balance of successes for the year was on the side of the Union. By the close of the year, 640,000 men had volunteered, not counting the 77,000 who came out under the first call. But the unaccountable inaction of McClellan's army filled the north with sorrow and doubt.—*U. S. in Am. Cy.*

1862. The war this year was so widely extended, and the events so numerous, that no detailed account can be given without occupying too much space. The following are the dates of some of the principal battles and events.

January 12th, Burnside's expedition sailed.

January 19th, Union victory at Mill Spring, Kentucky.

February 6th, Fort Henry, Tennessee, captured by Commodore Foote.

February 7th, General Burnside's expedition captured Roanoke Island.

February 16th, Fort Donelson and 16,000 men taken by General Grant.

February 24th, the rebels evacuated Nashville.

March 6th, McClellan's army in motion.

March 7th, Union victory of Pea Ridge, Arkansas.

March 9th, the iron-clad Merrimac and the Monitor meet, and the Monitor triumphs.

March 14th, Burnside took Newbern, North Carolina.

April 4th, McClellan advances on Yorktown, and opens the Peninsular Campaign.

April 6th and 7th, Battle of Shiloh, Tennessee.

April 25th, New Orleans captured.

May 4th, rebels evacuate Yorktown.

May 5th, Union victory at Williamsburg.

May 31st, Battle of Fair Oaks on the Chickahominy.

June 6th, rebel fleet destroyed and Memphis taken.

June 16th, Union repulse on James Island.

June 26th, General Pope assumed command of Army of Virginia.

June 27th, Battle of Gaine's Mills.

June 28th, Battle of White Oak Swamp.

July 1st, Battle of Malvern Hill.

July 1st, President calls for 300,000 more men.

August 29th, second Battle of Bull Run. Pope defeated.

September 5th, Lee invaded Maryland.

September 13th, Battle of South Mountain.

September 15th, Harper's Ferry surrendered to rebels.

September 27th, Battle of Antietam.

October 3d, Battle of Corinth.

November 7th, Burnside assumes command of Army of the Potomac.

December 13th, Battle of Fredericksburg.

December 31, the Battle of Stone River, Tennessee, began.

January 1st, President Lincoln issued his celebrated Proclamation emancipating the slaves in the rebel States.

1863. Mexico was rent by repeated revolutions and civil wars from the outset of its independence. In 1858, a new revolution compelled President Commonfort to resign. The Conservatives elected General Zuloaga, while Juarez, being Chief Justice of the Supreme Court, became, by the Constitution, President on the resignation of Commonfort. Zuloaga having been deposed, General Miramon became chief of the Conservatives, or Church party, and a civil war raged between his party and that of Juarez. In 1861, Spain, England, and France sent a combined force to enforce certain claims. Spain and England, having adjusted their claims, withdrew.

In 1862, the Church party sought the aid of foreign intervention, and a French force was sent into the country, and a war was waged between them and the Liberals.—*Annual Cy.*, 1862.

January 26th, General Hooker assumed command of the Army of the Potomac.

April 16th, a fleet of gunboats ran past Vicksburg.

April 20th, West Virginia was, by proclamation of the President, admitted to the Union.

May 1st–3d, Battle of Chancellorsville.

June 14th, the rebel army again crossed the Potomac and invaded Maryland and Pennsylvania.

June 28th, General Mead was put in command of the Army of the Potomac.

July 1st–3d, the great and decisive victory of Gettysburg.

July 4th, Vicksburg surrendered.

July 13th–16th, draft riots in New York and Brooklyn.

August 1st, General Burnside occupied Knoxville.

September 19th and 20th, Battle of Chicamauga.

Nov. 17th–Dec. 3d, Siege of Knoxville; Longstreet repulsed.

November 25th, Battle of Mission Ridge.

Operations against Fort Sumter and Charleston were carried on during the summer and autumn.

The Rebellion received such stunning blows this year that its final defeat became certain. The opening of the Mississippi cut it in twain, and greatly crippled its resources.

1864.

March 1st, General Grant was created Lieutenant General, and, on the 10th, assumed the chief command of all the Union armies, with "head quarters in the field."

During the spring months, General Banks' unfortunate Red River expedition was undertaken. He was finally driven back defeated.

April 12th, Fort Pillow was treacherously captured by General Forrest, and its garrison inhumanly massacred.

The chief operations of the year were Grant's march to Richmond, and Sherman's march from Chattanooga to the sea.

May 4th, Grant's advance crossed the Rapidan. Fighting began at once, and the terrible battles of the Wilderness soon followed, then Spottsylvania Court House with scarcely any intermission. Alternately fighting and flanking the enemy, Grant reached and crossed the James, and, after severe fighting, took position before Petersburg. Another campaign was conducted in the Shenandoah Valley, first under Sigel, but finally under Sheridan. The government, fully aroused, energetically supported all the operations, and the nation was full of energy and excitement.

About the time Grant crossed the Rapidan, Sherman left Chattanooga, and, by a brilliant series of battles, fought his way to Atlanta, which place surrendered the 1st of September. In November, Sherman, after sending the rebel General Hood into Tennessee, where Thomas was ready to meet him, cut loose from his base, and began his celebrated march to the sea, reaching Savannah, December 10th. In November and December, General Thomas beat Hood in the severe battles of Franklin and Nashville.—*Army Operations in Annual Cy. for* 1864. *Am. Conflict, Vol.* 2.

The French troops having, in 1863, defeated the Liberal army under Generals Commonfort and Ortega, proceeded to proclaim Maximilian of Austria, Emperor; but Maximilian declined, till, in April, 1864, being assured that the Mexican people, by vote, had given in their adhesion to the French rule, he embarked for Mexico, and, June 12th, made a grand entry into his capital, amid the cheers of the French and the apathetic silence of the natives. The war with Juarez still went on, and may yet end in driving Maximilian from the throne.—*Annual Cy. for* 1864.

January, General Sherman, leaving Savannah, began his north-
1865. ward march through the interior of South Carolina,
wading swamps, fighting, tearing up railroads, and scattering devastation. Columbia and Charleston were surrendered after being nearly burned up, the former by accident. Leaving a broad trail of desolation, the Union army swept in triumph into North Carolina till it reached and rested at Goldsborough, about the middle of March.

January 15th, another Union force, with a fleet of iron-clads, captured Fort Fisher, North Carolina, after a severe battle.

General Wilson, with a Union army, penetrated Alabama and captured Selma, April 2, and Montgomery, April 12th.

Grant still sat before Petersburg, slowly extending his lines around the doomed city, with occasional severe fights.

March 29th, the final movement began. Battle followed battle; victory followed victory, till, Sunday, April 2d. Petersburg fell, and the rebel government fled from Richmond.

April 9th, Lee's army surrendered at Appomattox Court House, Virginia.

For full account of the war during the years '62, '63, '64, and '65, see Annual Cyclopædias for those years, or Greeley's American Conflict, or any good History of the Great Rebellion.

April 14th, President Lincoln was assassinated. The nation melted to tears, and were shrouded in gloom. Perhaps no death on earth was ever so widely deplored as that of the great and good President, whose martyrdom closed the Great Rebellion of the slaveholders of America.

Andrew Johnson of Tennessee, the Vice-President, immediately assumed the duties of the Presidency.

April 26th, General Johnson surrendered the remaining rebel forces to General Sherman.

May 11th, Jefferson Davis, the fugitive rebel President, was captured near Irwinsville, Georgia.

But the grandest event of the year was the adoption of the Constitutional Amendment, abolishing slavery forever in the United States. Thus ended the long battle of opinion which had agitated American history during half a century like a great subterranean volcanic force, threatening the frequent and fatal overthrow of the Union.—*Am. Conflict, Vol. 2, p.* 673.

This year was occupied with the exciting discussions of the several plans for the reconstruction of the Union.

1866. But the event of most consequence in American history was the successful laying of the Atlantic Telegraph Cable, which brought the two Continents into immediate communication, and fitly crowned that long series of splendid triumphs of art which had made the century glorious. The cable was laid by a British ship and by British capital, but its triumph is due largely to the indomitable perseverence of that now eminent American, Cyrus W. Field.

The real history of our country during this great century lies not in the region of political movement, but in the march of moving populations, filling State after State, and adding constantly new empires to the ever-widening areas of Christian civilization; in the swift upward sweep of those great wealth-producing arts which are steadily elevating the sphere of human toil, from the low drudgery of the muscles to the rich and grander realms of thought-work; and in the amazing multiplication of those great agencies and elements of human elevation and progress, the free press, the pulpit, and the school—the educating powers which promise that this age, which has placed the people in power, shall vindicate in the higher intelligence, virtue, and culture of the race, the excellence of free government.

GREAT BRITAIN.

The opening of the Nineteenth Century found Great Britain engaged in a gigantic struggle with the First Consul and the French, with that grand and indomitable statesman, William Pitt, at the head of affairs; though in the second month of the century, he retired from his post, only to be recalled three years later.

The century has been one of great changes in the British Constitution, and of great advances in the material wealth and grandeur of England.

The English government insisting on its right of searching neutral vessels bound for the ports of France or any
1801. hostile nation, to see if they carried any articles contraband of war, Russia, Sweden, and Denmark entered into a treaty to resist, by force of arms, this pretended right of search. To oppose this armed neutrality, Lord Nelson, with a British fleet, attacked Copenhagen, and destroyed the Danish fleet.—*Modern Eu., Vol.* 3, *pp.* 421, 422. *Pict. Eng., Vol.* 6, *p.* 154 *and pp.* 161, 162.

March 27th, the Peace of Amiens closed the great and terrible war between France and England, and gave peace
1802. for a short time to Europe.—*Mod. Eu., Vol.* 3, *p.* 427.

In May, the flame of war with France again broke out, and the conflagration speedily swept over Europe. The
1803. year was full of fighting. The peace had been a mere truce. The great battle was to be fought out.—*Mod. Eu., Vol.* 3, *p*, 472.

A powerful confederacy of the Mahratta chiefs having been made in Hindostan against the English power, a fierce and bloody war broke out. After severe and brilliant fighting throughout the Deccan, under General Arthur Wellesley, afterwards Duke of Wellington, the English triumphed, and another large territory was added to their East Indian Empire.—*Hindostan in Am. Cy.*

The union of Ireland and England, effected in 1800, met with great opposition from many Irish patriots. Robert Emmett attempted a revolution, but was caught, tried, and executed. The Irish still cherish his memory.—*Emmett in Am. Cy. Pict. Eng., Vol.* 6, *pp.* 214–217.

The gigantic struggle, now taxing all the energies of England, compelled the recall of Pitt, and, May 12th, he again
1804. became Prime Minister.—*Pict. Eng., Vol.* 6, *pp.* 230, 231.

A war with Spain was begun this year.

The Third Coalition was formed against the overshadowing power of France, first by England and Russia, and after-
1805. wards joined by Sweden and Austria.—*Mod. Eu., Vol.* 3, *p.* 488.

In October, the great naval victory over the combined fleets of France and Spain, was won by Lord Nelson, who was killed in the hour of victory.—*Mod. Eu., Vol.*, 3, *p.* 493.

The Third Coalition being crushed by the victory of Austerlitz, a fourth was speedily formed, embracing England,
1806. Russia, Prussia, Saxony, and Sweden.—*Mod. Eu., Vol.* 3, *pp.* 496, 497.

Pitt died, January 23d, and a ministry was formed under Lord Grenville, in which was included Pitt's old foeman, the celebrated orator, Charles James Fox. Fox died in the following September.—*Pitt and Fox in Am. Cy. Mod. Eu. Vol.* 3, *pp.* 497, 498, *and p.* 506.

The Berlin Decree, issued by Napoleon, November 20th, interdicted all commerce with Great Britain, and forbade all vessels which touched at English ports from entering any port under French control.—*Mod. Eu., Vol.* 3, *p*, 510.

June 11th, under the lead of Fox, and of that great philanthropist, William Wilberforce, the long struggle for the abolition of the slave trade won its first triumph in Parliament by the passage of an act forbidding the exportation of slaves from British Colonies after January 1st, 1807.—*Pict. Eng., Vol.* 6, *p.* 315. *Mod. Eu., Vol.* 3, *p.* 499.

The Berlin Decree, which had been provoked by the English
1807. orders in Council, was answered by another order in
Council prohibiting all coast trade with France. America and other neutral powers suffered greatly from these measures.—*Lossing's U. S., p.* 401.

England took another step this year in humanity, and abolished the African slave trade, the traffic to cease after January 1st, 1808.—*Pict Eng., Vol.* 6, *p.* 356.

The war with France and Spain raged through this year in Egypt, in South America, and around the coast of Europe. September 2nd–5th, Copenhagen was furiously bombarded by the British fleet and forced to surrender. This drew the power of both Denmark and Russia down upon England.—*Mod. Eu., Vol.* 3, *pp.* 518–522.

Napoleon having placed his brother Joseph on the throne of
1808. Spain, England sent an army to Spain to aid the anti-French party. The British under Sir John Moore suffered many defeats.—*Mod. Eu., Vol.* 3, *pp.* 527, 534.

Sir Arthur Wellesley was sent to take command of the British
1809. forces in Spain and Portugal, and entered upon the second campaign of the long Peninsular War.

George III. again became insane, and, December 20th, his
1810. son George, Prince of Wales, was appointed Regent by act of Parliament.—*Pict. Eng., Vol.* 6, 564.

The aggressions of England on American commerce led to a
1812. declaration of war between the two countries. See dates under "America." The Peninsular War was still raging in Spain with great fury.—*Mod. Eu., Vol.* 3, *pp.* 570–574.

Napoleon's power being broken by his disastrous Russian
1813. campaign, a Grand Coalition was formed against him, and an immense allied force was put in the field to check and, finally, to drive him from power.—*Napoleon in Am. Cy.*

In the world-renowned battle of Waterloo, won chiefly by Eng-
1815. lish arms under Wellington, the long struggle of England against the French culminated. England had triumphed. Her great foeman, the mighty Napoleon, fell, finally, into her hands.—*Waterloo in Am. Cy. Mod. Eu., Vol.*, 3, *pp.* 629–634.

In 1817, the princess Charlotte, the heiress to the British crown, died. The Pindaree and Mahratta wars in India also occurred this year.

1819. The English people had not been insensible to the spirit of the age demanding recognition of the inherent rights of the movements begun early in the century to secure an extension of the right of sufferage, and "Parliamentary Reform" became the watch word of the liberal, or "radical," party in England.

August 16th, a monster reform meeting, assembled at Manchester, was dispersed by a military force, many of the people being needlessly killed or wounded. This gave deeper earnestness and power to the agitation.—*Pict. Eng., Vol.* 7. *pp.* 104–110.

1820. The aged George III. died in the 60th year of his reign, and his son, George IV., already regent, became king.—*George III. and George IV. in Am. Cy.*

1823. A motion made in Parliament condemning slavery, and expressing a hope of its final abolition, created as great an excitement among the slaveholders in the West Indies as was afterwards seen in the United States. They threatened separation, and mobbed the missionaries among them.—*Pict. Eng. Vol.* 7, *pp.* 168–170.

1824. In 1823, the Burmese government opened a quarrel with the British, and, in 1824, declared war. The English sent a force which penetrated and desolated the country. The war closed in 1826, and a large strip of the coast of Burmah was ceded to England.—*Pict. Eng., Vol.* 7, *pp.* 154, 155.

1827. The Turks and Greeks having been at war for some years, England, France, and Russia formed an alliance to interfere and prevent further hostilities. An allied fleet blockaded the combined Turkish and Egyptian fleets in the harbor of Navarino. October 20th, the Battle of Navarino was brought on without design, and resulted in the entire destruction of the Turkish and Egyptian fleets.—*Greece in Am. Cy.*

1829. One of the great agitating questions in English politics during this century, was that of the emancipation of the Catholics from the legal provision which excluded them from office. The election, in 1828, of Daniel O'Connell, an Irish Catholic, as a member of Parliament, urged the long controversy to a conclusion. In 1829, the Catholic Relief bill was brought forward by Sir Robert Peel, and finally passed, admitting the great Irish agitator to Parliament.—*Pict. Eng., Vol.* 7, *p.* 259.

June 26th, the poor, unhappy, debauched George IV. died,
and was succeeded by his brother as William IV.—
1830. *William IV. in Am. Cy.*

The Reform movement had steadily grown in power from the
bloody day at Manchester. March 1st, Lord John
1831. Russell, in behalf of the ministry, brought forward a
Reform Bill in the House of Commons. It was defeated in Parliament, but the king dissolved the Parliament, and the great question went to the people for a new election.—*Pict. Eng., Vol.* 7, *pp.* 340–348.

England rocked with excitement. The Reform Party triumphed. When the new Parliament assembled the bill was again proposed, and, on the 21st of September, passed the Commons. It was, however, defeated in the House of Lords.

The defeat of the Reform Bill was followed by great excitement throughout England, and a civil war seemed threat-
1832. ening. A new Reform bill had been introduced into the
Commons, December 12th, 1831, and passed by a large majority. May 7th, 1832, the largest meeting ever yet assembled in England, 150,000 people, met at Birmingham. The people were fully aroused. The military were preparing to meet them. England stood on the brink of a great Revolution. The Grey ministry resigned. May 14th, a larger meeting of 200,000 people met at Manchester. May 15th, Lord Grey returned to power. The iron Duke of Wellington and the Peers gave way. June 4th, the Reform bill passed the Lords, and, June 7th, it became a law by the royal assent. England was revolutionized and saved.—*Pict., Eng. Vol.* 7, *pp.* 355–365.

Sir Robert Peel was made Prime Minister, but the Conservatives were in the minority, and, after a struggle of five
1834. months, he was compelled to resign. This was his first
Premiership.—*Peel in Am. Cy.*

A bill abolishing slavery passed Parliament in August, 1833, but did not take effect till August 1st, 1834. Freedom thus took another step forward in England.—*Slavery in Am. Cy.*

Lord Melbourne, who had been a member of Lord Grey's ministry and succeeded him for a short time, was now re-
1835. stored to power, and remained at the head of affairs till
1841.—*Melbourne in Am. Cy.*

William IV. died, June 20th, and was succeeded by his neice,
Victoria, the present excellent Queen of Great Britain,
1837. then only eighteen years of age. As the Hanoverian
law forbade the succession of a female, the crown of Hanover
now fell into the hands of the Duke of Cumberland, a younger
brother of William IV.—*Victoria in Am. Cy.*

The Reform Bill of 1832, did not close the progress of the
reform movements. The working men gained nothing
1838. by that bill. The agitation now recommenced among
the working classes, the agitators being called Chartists, from
the "Charter," or bill of rights proposed by them. In the latter
part of 1838, immense torch-light meetings were held in the
north of England, and, early in the next year, the movement
broke out into riots. Chartism was soon suppressed, to break
out at a later day.—*Chartism in Am. Cy.*

The Chinese government, in order to abolish the ruinous use
of opium by its subjects, had prohibited the importation
1839. of that article. The British merchants persisted in
sending cargoes of it, and soon a destructive war broke out.
After many defeats, the Chinese government consented to peace
in 1842. This war opened China more fully to foreign trade.—
Pict. Eng, Vol. 7, pp. 615–617.

February 10th, Queen Victoria was married to Prince Albert,
Duke of Saxe Coburg Gotha.—*Albert in Am. Cy.*
1840.

The Melbourne Whig ministry was at last compelled to resign,
and Sir Robert Peel again came into power with a Con-
1841. servative Cabinet. The repeal of the Corn Laws, so as
to admit breadstuffs to be imported free of duty, was the question
now agitating all England.—*Pict. Eng., Vol. 7, pp.* 607–609.

O'Connell, "the Great Agitator," had years before raised the cry for the repeal of the union of Ireland and England.
1843. This year, he instigated monster meetings all over Ireland, some of them estimated as high as 500,000 persons. The whole country rung with the cry of Repeal. The agitation died with O'Connell's death, in 1847.—*O'Connell in Am. Cy. Pict. Eng., Vol.* 7, *pp.* 657–667.

The great agitation triumphed; the Corn Laws were repealed, June 26th. Soon after, that great statesman, Sir Robert
1846. Peel resigned the Premiership he had so ably held, and was succeeded by Lord John Russell, who continued in office till 1852.—*Peel and Russell in Am. Cy.*

The great industrial exhibition, called the World's Fair, was held in London under the direction of Prince Albert.—
1851. *Albert in Am. Cy.*

Russia, threatening the absorption of Turkey; England, France, and Sardinia interfered on the side of Turkey, on the
1854. plea that the continued existence of Turkey was necessary to the peace of Europe. The Crimean war, which followed, was chiefly famous for the siege of Sebastopol.—*Russia and Turkey in Am. Cy.*

Sebastopol was taken by the allies after an active and bloody siege of eleven months.—*Crimea in Am. Cy.*
1855. On the retirement of Lord Aberdeen from the Premiership, Lord Palmerston was made Prime Minister.—*Palmerston in Am. Cy.*

The English, on some slight pretence, opened a war with China by a bombardment of Canton. The French
1856. united in these hostilities, and, afterwards, the United States and Russia interfered. The war continued till 1858.—*China in Am. Cy.*

The Sepoy soldiers, who constituted a large part of the British force in Hindostan, mutinied, and raised the standard of
1857. revolt, butchering the English residents in great numbers. The revolt rapidly extended through the whole of Bengal, and was only suppressed after three years of severe fighting, and the destruction of large numbers of the natives with unsparing

severity. The Siege of Lucknow by the Sepoys, and of Delhi by the English, were among the most celebrated scenes of this awful outburst of savage passion. In consequence of this war the government of India was transferred from the India Company to the home government, and Queen Victoria became Queen of Hindostan.—*Hindostan, Lucknow, and Delhi in Am. Cy.*

In 1858, Palmerston's ministry was overthrown, and the Derby
ministry succeeded, but, in June, 1859, Palmerston again
1859. became Premier, with Russell as Secretary of State for
foreign affairs.—*Palmerston and Russell in Am. Cy.*

October 18th, the veteran Palmerston died. A new ministry
was immediately formed, with Earl Russell as Prime
1865. Minister, and Gladstone, the foremost of the living English statesmen, as Chancellor of the Exchequer.—*Anl. Cy.* 1865.

In July, the Derby Ministry came into power. England has
made immense strides in territory, wealth, and power
1866. during this century, as well as in the freedom and intelligence of her people.

FRANCE.

The Nineteenth Century shows no more brilliant or remarkable history than that of France. At the dawn of this century the nation lay, crushed in liberty, but tremendous in strength, in the hand of the First Consul, Napoleon Bonaparte. The mightiest nations of Europe trembled at the resistless energy of the French soldiers led by this wonderful general. For fifteen years the old dynasties struggled against the Corsican and his Frenchmen, and not till the whole continent rose in insurrection against him could they throw off his yoke. Fifteen years more ripened France for another revolution, and only a little more than this period added, brought the revolution of '48, which resulted only as the first did, in bringing a Bonaparte to the throne, and placing France in the van of historic movements.

January 26th, the Republic of Italy made Bonaparte President

1802. for ten years : Bonaparte's success having compelled the
other powers to make peace ; England also sullenly con-
sented, and the Peace of Amiens was signed, March 27th.—*Pict. Eng., Vol.* 6, *p.* 172. *Amiens in Am. Cy.*

In August, Bonaparte was named First Consul for life.—*Mod. Eu., Vol.* 3, *p.* 462. *Bonaparte in Am. Cy.*

England could not forgive France nor Napoleon, and the Eng-
1803. lish government believed that the invasion of England
was a life-long project of Bonaparte. The seas around Europe at once swarmed with English ships, and the land bristled with French bayonets. The mutual jealousies of France and England soon led to a renewal of war. England never ceased from this war till Napoleon was driven from the throne. —*Mod. Eu., Vol.* 3, *p.* 472.

May 18th, Napoleon was declared Emperor of the French.
1804. The coronation took place December 2d.—*Bonaparte in*
Am. Cy. Mod. Eu., Vol. 3, *pp.* 479, 480.

England succeeded in forming a Third Coalition against
1805. France, and soon the armies of Russia and Austria were
again in motion.—*Mod. Eu., Vol.* 3, *p.* 488.

But the genius of Napoleon was equal to the emergency. October 20th, an Austrian army surrendered in Ulm. November 13th, the French entered Vienna. December 2d, Napoleon met the combined Russian and Austrian armies at Austerlitz, and gained a great and decisive victory. The Emperors of Russia and Austria were both present in this battle, which crushed the Coalition and compelled Austria to make the Peace of Presburg.—*Mod. Eu., Vol.* 3, *pp.* 489, 490. *Austerlitz in Am. Cy.*

The Battle of Trafalgar, so disastrous to the French navy, occurred October 21st.

Napoleon now commenced giving away crowns. March 30th,
1806. he declared his brother Joseph King of Naples. June
5th, he placed his brother Louis on the throne of Holland. July 12th, fourteen of the German States formed the Confederation of the Rhine and chose Napoleon Protector.—*Mod. Eu., Vol.* 3, *p.* 496.

Prussia now joined the enemies of Napoleon, and, without waiting for allies, declared war, October 9th. Napoleon was already in the field. October 14th, was fought the great Battle of Jena, in which the French gained a decisive victory. October 25th, the French army entered Berlin. The several corps of the Prussian army surrendered within a few days after this.

From Berlin, Napoleon issued his Berlin Decree against the commerce of England.—*Mod. Eu., Vol.* 3, *pp.* 509, 510.

Russia had now entered the field. February 7th and 8th, was
1807. fought the desperate Battle of Eylau, in which the victory was claimed by both parties. June 14th, Napoleon won the decisive victory of Friedland. July 7th, the Peace of Tilsit was concluded between Napoleon and Alexander, and, a few days later, between France and Prussia.—*Mod. Eu., Vol.* 3, *pp.* 511–513.

The English Order in Council, issued in retaliation of the Berlin Decree, called out the Milan Decree.—*Lossing's U. S.*

Napoleon, taking advantage of internal dissensions in Spain,
1808. seized the throne for his brother Joseph, and gave the crown of Naples to his brother-in-law, Murat.—*Mod. Eu., Vol.* 3, *p.* 527. *Napoleon Bonaparte in Am. Cy.*

Austria again entered into the war still waged by England.
1809. The campaign opened in April. April 22d, the French gained a victory at Eckmuhl, and captured Ratisbon, and, on the 10th of May, Napoleon again entered Vienna as conqueror. On the 22d, Napoleon suffered a crushing defeat at Esling; but, on the 6th and 7th of July, he gained the great and hard-fought Battle of Wagram, and, in October, the Peace of Vienna closed the campaign.—*Mod. Eu., Vol.* 3, *pp.* 538–540.

In December, Napoleon took that wicked and fatal step, the divorce of his faithful wife, the Empress Josephine.—*Josephine in Am. Cy. Mod. Eu., Vol.* 3, *p.* 558.

March 11th, Napoleon married Maria Louisa, the daughter of
1810. Francis I., emperor of Austria. One year later, a son was born to him, and his power seemed permanent. His star now culminated.

Napoleon entered upon his great and fatal Russian campaign

1812. with an army of nearly half a million men. Fighting the Battle of Smolensko, with many minor ones, the French pressed forward, and, after the tremendous contest of Borodino, captured Moscow, which the inhabitants abandoned. Two days after the French entered the city, it was set on fire by the Russians and burned. Napoleon, thus robbed of his winter quarters, was compelled to retreat. Thousands of his soldiers perished by cold and by Cossack lances, and he emerged from the Russian snows with a mere fragment of his great army.—*Mod. Au., Vol.* 3, *pp.* 588–596. *Borodino in Am. Cy.*

Europe took heart again, after seeing the issue of the Russian
1813. Campaign, and formed a Sixth Grand Coalition to beat back the overwhelming power of France. Napoleon, rallying a new army, boldly advanced against the immense hosts which were mustering to crush him. October 16th–19th, the great Battle of Leipsic was fought. The French were finally beaten and forced to retreat across the Rhine.—*Mod. Eu., Vol.* 3, *p.* 599. *Leipsic in Am. Cy.*

The allies now broke into France on all sides. Wellington,
1814. victorious in Spain, entered France from the South. The Austrians invaded Italy, and the great armies crossed the Rhine. Napoleon displayed immense activity, and won several victories, but he could not prevent the catastrophe. The allies entered Paris, March 31st. He was forced to abdicate, and was banished to Elba. The Bourbons, after so many years of exile, were restored, and Louis XVIII., the brother of the unfortunate Louis XVI., was placed on the throne.—*Mod. Eu., Vol.* 3, *pp.* 601–603. *White's France, pp.* 512–516.

March 1st, Napoleon, escaping from Elba, landed in France,
1815. and took up his march with a thousand men for Paris. March 20th, he entered his capital in triumph, at the head of a great army. The great powers of Europe now armed at once for the inevitable conflict. June 14th, Napoleon quit Paris and put himself at the head of his army in Belgium. After gaining the victory of Ligny, he was finally and fatally defeated in the world-renowned Battle of Waterloo, fought the 18th of June.

This closed the reign of the "Hundred Days." Napoleon again abdicated, and was banished to the island of St. Helena, where he died in 1821.—*Mod. Eu., Vol.* 3, *pp.* 618–634. *Bonaparte, and Waterloo in Am. Cy. White's France, pp.* 521–528.

The allied armies were this year withdrawn from Paris, and
1818. the French king acceded to the Holy Alliance which
had been formed by the monarchs of Russia, Austria,
and Prussia while in Paris in 1815.—*Mod. Eu., Vol.* 3, *p.* 645.

Paris was full of factions. The Duc de Berri, the nephew of the
1820. king and the second in succession to the crown, was
murdered by a Bonapartist assassin.—*Mod. Eu., Vol.* 3,
p. 652. *Berry, Charles Ferdinand, Duke of, in Am Cy.*

A French army entered Spain under the sanction of the Holy
1823. Alliance, suppressed the Liberal party, and restored the
miserable king to his throne.—*Mod. Eu., Vol.* 3, *p.* 662.

Louis XVIII. died, September 15th, and was succeeded by
1824. his brother, Charles X., a prince whose despotic temper
soon aroused again in France the old revolutionary feeling.—*White's France, p.* 536. *Charles X. in Am. Cy.*

The arbitrary measures of Charles X. at length caused an
1830. armed revolt, and the Three Days' Revolution of July
drove him from his throne, and seated in his place Louis Philippe, Duke of Orleans. Louis Philippe sympathized with the popular feeling, assumed the title of Citizen King, and succeeded in consolidating his power.—*White's France, pp.* 540–543. *Louis Philippe in Am. Cy.*

Louis Napoleon, nephew of the great Napoleon, relying upon
1836. the power of the name he bore, proclaimed a revolution
at Strasburg. A few soldiers of the garrison joined him; but he was soon taken prisoner and banished to the United States, his attempt being counted as a freak of folly or insanity. —*White's France, p.* 545. *Bonaparte, Louis Nap. in Am. Cy.*

In 1840, he made another attempt to excite revolution at Boulogne, but failed, and, after being imprisoned, escaped to England, where he devoted himself to literary pursuits till the Revolution of '48.

Louis Philippe, false to his professions, gradually grew tyranni-

cal, till the old revolutionary spirit being again roused in
1848. Paris, he was driven, February 28th, 1848, from his throne, and the French Republic proclaimed. All Europe was rife with revolution.—*Louis Philippe, and Bonaparte, Louis Napoleon in Am. Cy. White's France, p.* 552.

Louis Napoleon, hearing of the Revolution, repaired at once to France, and was elected a deputy to the National Assembly. In December, he was elected President of the Republic for the term of four years.—*France, and Bonaparte Louis Nap., in Am. Cy.*

A French army entered Rome, suppressed the new Roman Republic, and restored the Pope to power. The French
1849. soldiers continued in Rome as an army of occupation till December, 1866.

Louis Napoleon, by a bold stroke, dissolved the Assembly, put down opposition by force, and, appealing to the
1851. people, was elected President for ten years.

The question of the re-establishment of the Empire having been presented to the people, and voted by a large
1852. majority, Louis Napoleon was, December 2d, proclaimed Emperor, as Napoleon III. Under his masterly rule, France speedily rose again to the rank of the first of the great continental powers of Europe.—*France in Am. Cy.*

France bore a conspicuous part in the Crimean war, and the French soldiery exhibited their old traits of enthusiastic
1854. and irresistable bravery.—*Crimea in Am. Cy.*

In the war which broke out in April, between Sardinia and Austria, and which became a war for the liberation of
1859. Italy, the French monarch took a leading part, leading a French army to assist Sardinia.—*Sardinian States, and Italy in Am. Cy.*

France, England, and Spain, in 1861, sent a combined fleet to Mexico to enforce certain claims held by each of these
1862. governments against the Mexicans. The English and Spaniards, having secured some adjustment of their claims, withdrew in April, 1862, and left the French alone in Mexico. They were soon reinforced, and began the conquest of the country.—*Mexico, and France in Annual Cy. for* 1862.

The astute and mysterious Napoleon still rules, and France is enjoying a large measure of quiet and prosperity under his reign. Arts and science flourish and advance with gigantic strides.

SPAIN AND PORTUGAL.

THESE two countries have suffered largely and profited little by these great struggles of the Nineteenth Century.

Spain, having been drawn into an alliance with France and a consequent war with England, lost twelve ships of war
1805. in the great Battle of Trafalgar.—*Spain in Am. Cy.*

The opposition to Godoy, the Premier of Spain, led to an insurrection, which compelled Charles IV. to abdicate in
1808. favor of his son, who became Ferdinand VII. But, attempting afterwards to recall his abdication, both father and son appealed to Napoleon, who gave the throne to his brother Joseph.—*Spain in Am. Cy.*

An insurrection against the French immediately broke out, and the Spaniards, supported by England, began that long struggle against France which only closed when Napoleon was hurled from his throne in 1813. The French were not finally expelled till 1814. This war for independence kindled some love of liberty, and a liberal Constitution was framed by the Spanish Cortes, or National Assembly, in 1812.—*Spain in Am. Cy.*

Revolutions broke out in both Spain and Portugal, the armies co-operating with the people. In Spain, the revolution
1820. compelled Ferdinand VII. to restore the Constitution of 1812, to assemble the Cortes, and to abolish the Inquisition. In Portugal, a liberal Constitution was adopted, and the royal family, which had fled to Brazil in 1808, was invited to return.—*Ferdinand VII., Spain, and Portugal in Am. Cy.*

John VI. of Portugal returned from Brazil, leaving his son,

Don Pedro, at the head of the Brazilian government.
1821. The next year, Don Pedro was declared Emperor of Brazil, and that country became independent.—*Spain, and Portugal in Am. Cy.*.

The struggle continuing in Spain between the Cortes and the King, the French sent an army to suppress the Cortes
1823. and restore Ferdinand to the throne.—*Spain in Am. Cy.*

Ferdinand VII. died, September 29th, and was succeeded by his daughter, Isabella. Her uncle, Don Carlos, also
1833. claimed the throne. Isabella was supported by the English, and the civil war which arose, only closed in 1839, with the final defeat of the Carlists.—*Isabella II. in Am. Cy.*

Another revolution broke out the same year, and, at intervals since, revolutionary movements have occurred.

GERMANY, PRUSSIA, AND AUSTRIA.

Austria reeled into the Nineteenth Century staggering under the blows dealt her by the French at Marengo and Hohenlinden. By the Peace of Luneville, concluded the 9th of February, the Austrian monarch ceded all his Italian possessions except Venetia, and Germany lost all west of the Rhine. Prussia, lying remote from the scene of war, had taken but little part in the struggle. The sacrifice of her territories across the Rhine was compensated by the accession to her domain of some small German States.

Francis II., Emperor of Germany, now took the title of Francis I., Emperor of Austria, and, two years later, he
1804. renounced entirely the German imperial crown. Austria was only partly German.—*Francis II. in Am. Cy.*

Austria, offended by Napoleon's violations of the treaty of Luneville, joined the Coalition with Russia and Eng-
1805. land. Prussia refused to join in this Coalition. A sharp and sudden campaign defeated the forces of the Coalition

at Ulm and Austerlitz, and Francis gladly made the treaty of Presburg, on Christmas day, yielding up another large slice of territory.—*Kohlrausch, pp.* 431–433.

July 12th, the German States lying near the Rhine formally
1806. separated themselves from the old Empire, and formed
the Confederation of the Rhine, with Napoleon as Protector.

The king of Prussia, finding himself cheated by France, now rushed into war, but Napoleon, advancing with great celerity, defeated his armies at Auerstadt and Jena, and entered his capital as conqueror. The Russians, who had formed with Prussia and other States the Fourth Coalition, entered the field. —*Kohlrausch, pp.* 434–436.

In February was fought the Battle of Eylau. After a com-
1807. parative quiet of nearly four months, fighting recom-
menced, ending in the hard-fought Battle of Friedland, in which the French gained, June 12th, a great victory. Napoleon soon took the last of the Prussian towns, and, in July, concluded with the Emperor Alexander and Frederick William, the Peace of Tilsit, in which he stripped the latter of more than half of his dominions, carving off a Duchy of Warsaw on the east, and the kingdom of Westphalia for his brother Jerome, on the west. Prussia was thoroughly humbled and took no further part in the wars for several years, except to furnish troops to Napoleon.—*Fred. Wm. III. in Am. Cy.* *Kohlrausch, pp.* 436, 437. *Gould's Allison's Europe, pp.* 205–218.

Austria, alarmed by Napoleon's successive grasps of power,
1809. entered into another Coalition with England and with
Spain and Portugal, now in revolt against France, and opened, the third time, a war against Napoleon. The events of the campaign have been given under "France." The Austrians fought with great valor and won several victories; but in the end, after the fatal Battle of Wagram, Francis was obliged, at the Peace of Vienna, to make another great sacrifice of territory. —*Kohlrausch, pp.* 438–441. *Gould's Allison's Eu., pp.* 253–268

Prince Metternich, long known as one of the ablest diplomatists and statesmen of Europe, became minister of foreign affairs in Austria this year. He continued in power till 1848.—*Metternich in Am. Cy.*

The Austrian and Prussian armies had both followed the
French standard in the Russian Campaign; but the
1813. Russians, in their pursuit of the fugitive army, took Berlin, and Prussia went over to Russia. The German States rose in insurrection against the French, and the Grand Coalition was formed; even Sweden and Austria united in it. The war that followed has already been related under "France." The triumph of the allied powers, in this and the following campaign, gave back to Austria and Prussia their possessions, and the Confederation of the Rhine ceased to exist. A new Confederation of German States was formed with a Diet at Frankfort. In this Diet, Austria held the presidency.—*Kohlrausch, pp.* 443–473. *Gould's Allison's Eu., pp.* 336–368.

In the grand final campaign against Napoleon, the Prussian
troops under Blucher bore an important part.
1815. While at Paris, in September, the emperors of Russia and Austria and the king of Prussia made a league, called the Holy Alliance, in which they declared that the political relations of Europe were to be founded on the Gospel. This Alliance used its powers in after years to suppress every appearance o free government.—*Holy Alliance in Am. Cy. Pict. Eng., Vol.* 7, *pp.* 2, 3.

A great Congress of the crowned heads of Europe was held at
Aix la Chapelle, in September. The chief business was
1818. to recall the allied army of occupation from France.—*Pict. Eng., Vol.* 7, *pp.* 93, 94.

Francis I. of Austria died, March 2d, and was succeeded by
his son, Ferdinand I., a prince of imbecile character,
1835. who was but little else than a puppet in the hands of his prime minister, the astute Metternich.—*Ferdinand I., ana Metternich in Am. Cy.*

On the death of Frederick William III. of Prussia, June 7th,
he was succeeded by his son, Frederick William IV., a
1840. talented, but vacillating and vindictive, king. Prussia had enjoyed a long peace, and its people had made great progress

in science and education.—*Frederick William IV. in Am. Cy.*

The revolutions of '48, which shook nearly every throne in
1848. Europe, were the result of many causes, mostly, perhaps, of the silent but steady progress of ideas of democratic liberty among the people. All Europe helped to hasten the catastrophe. Some partial concessions made by Frederick William IV. and by Pope Pius IX. fanned the flame, and various local difficulties added to its intensity. The French Revolution, which broke out in February and resulted in the establishment of a Republic, sent an electric shock throughout the Continent. In Baden, Wurtemberg, Saxony, and other German States, the Liberal party came into power and the demands of the people were granted.

In Vienna, a violent uprising of the populace drove Metternich into exile, and finally compelled the weak Ferdinand to yield his throne to his nephew, Francis Joseph.

In Prussia great commotions occurred and the king finally granted a liberal Constitution, which he afterwards violated. In Italy violent disturbances arose. Rome became a Republic and the Pope fled in dismay. Tuscany revolted and formed a short-lived Republic. Milan and Venice drove out the Austrians, but were reduced again to obedience.—*Frederick William IV. in Am. Cy.*

Hungary, encouraged by the general revolt, struck for independence of the Austrian rule, and made Louis Kossuth Provisional Governor.—*Weber's Outlines, pp.* 518–526. *Austria, Hungary, Germany, Italy, Francis Joseph, Kossuth in Am. Cy.*

The monarchs who had yielded to the popular will, having
1849. treacherously gained power, soon began to recall their concessions and to banish the leading Liberals.

The French interfered and restored the Pope to Rome. The Russians coming to the aid of Austria, Gorgey, the Hungarian general, surrendered his army, and Kossuth and the other leaders fled. The new German Empire was put down by the Prussian army.—*Weber's Outlines, pp.* 526–530.—*Frederick William IV. in Am. Cy.*

Prussia attempted to gain an ascendency among the German

1850. States and to exclude Austria from Germany, but Austria, forming an alliance with the southern German States, defeated the plan, and returned to its place in the Diet at Frankfort.—*Frederick William IV., and Francis Joseph in Am. Cy.*

By the war for the liberation of Italy, Austria lost all her
1859. Italian possessions except Venetia.

Frederick William IV. having abdicated the throne, his
1861. brother, William I, succeeded.—*William I. in Am. Cy.*

The German Duchies of Schleswig and Holstein had been
1864. united with Denmark for a long period, though several times struggling for independence. On the death of the king, Frederick VII. of Denmark, in 1863, several claimants appeared. The Duchies appealed to Germany to be released from the Danish yoke, and a war was begun. Finally, in February, Austria and Prussia sent their allied forces, which defeated the Danes and compelled them to relinquish the Duchies in the Peace of Vienna, October 30th.

Austria and Prussia quarrelled over the possession of the
1866. Duchies, and war finally broke out between them. Both parties made immense preparations as if for a death grapple. The Prussians gained repeated victories, and finally dealt upon Austria the crushing defeat of Sadowa. The Austrians were compelled to a peace, in which they relinquished large territories to Prussia, and also gave up Venetia, nearly their last possession in Italy. This war greatly increased the power of Prussia, and seems likely to issue in the re-establishment of the German Empire with a Prussian head.

HOLLAND AND BELGIUM.

THE French Revolution early affected the Netherlands, and, in 1795, Holland having been conquered by the French, the whole country was organized into the Batavian Republic.

The Batavian Republic was transformed by Napoleon into the
Kingdom of Holland, and his brother Louis was made
1806. king.—*Gould's Allison, p.* 196. *Netherlands in Am. Cy.*

After the fall of Napoleon, the Prince of Orange was proclaimed king, under the title of William I.—*Neth. in Am. Cy.*

The ten provinces known as the Spanish or Austrian Netherlands, having revolted from the Kingdom of Holland,
1831. established the Kingdom of Belgium, with Leopold I., a
prince of Saxe-Coburg, as king.—*Leopold I., and Netherlands in Am. Cy.*

Holland and Belgium continue separate kingdoms, and are enjoying a peaceful and prosperous history under their respective sovereigns.

ITALY.

ITALY holds a prominent place in the history of the Nineteenth Century. The opening of the century found Venice under the control of Austria, and Lombardy and Parma under the French, bearing the name of the Cisalpine Republic.

The Cisalpine was transformed into the Italian Republic, and
Napoleon was chosen President. In 1805, it became
1802. the Kingdom of Italy, and several new provinces were
absorbed in it.—*Italy in Am. Cy.*

Napoleon made his brother Joseph king of the Two Sicilies,
(Naples and Sicily). The remainder of the Italian
1806. States were apportioned among Napoleon's sisters and
his chief officers.—*Gould's Allison's Europe, p.* 195. *Italy in Am. Cy.*

When Joseph was transferred to the throne of Spain, Joachim
Murat, one of Napoleon's generals and his brother-in-
1808. law, was made king of Naples in his stead. On the fall
of Napoleon, in 1814, Murat, who had taken sides with the allies, was dethroned.—*Murat, and Italy in Am. Cy.*

On the downfall of Napoleon, in 1814, Victor Emanuel I. of
Sardinia reappeared in Piedmont and resumed his sway.
1821. In 1821, a military insurrection induced him to abdicate
in favor of his brother Charles Felix.

Charles Albert succeeded Charles Felix on the throne of Sardinia. He was a prince of liberal principles.—*Sardinian*
1831. *States, and Charles Albert in Am. Cy.*

Pius IX., the present (1867) Pope of Rome, was elected to the
Papal chair in June. 1846. His known liberal views
1846. caused his accession to be hailed with joy by the people.
—*Pius IX. in Am. Cy.*

The liberal concessions of Pius IX., in 1847, served to set on
fire the revolutionary sentiment which had long been
1848. gathering throughout Europe. The outburst came in
France in February, 1848, and rapidly spread. In Rome, it
speedily outran the views of the Pope, and, in November, 1848,
he fled from Rome and a Republic was established.—*Pius IX.
in Am. Cy.*

The Pope calling upon the Catholic powers for armed assistance, France sent a force which entered Rome, July 1st,
1849. and suppressed the Republic. The French troops continued in Rome to protect the Pope till December, 1866.

Charles Albert of Sardinia put himself at the head of the popular movement in northern Italy; but being fatally defeated at Novara, he resigned the crown to his son, Victor Emanuel II., the present king of Italy.—*Victor Emanuel, and Pius IX. in Am Cy.*

In the war for the liberation of Italy from Austrian rule, Victor
Emanuel was aided by France and by Garibaldi. This
1859. war, with the subsequent revolutions in which the popu-
lar votes were given for union with Sardinia, gave to Victor
Emanuel the kingdom of United Italy.—*Garibaldi, and Italy in
Am. Cy, and in Annual Cy.*

Italy was allied with Prussia in the short but eventful war of
this summer. Austria was obliged, in the peace made
1866. August 22d, to yield Venetia, and now retains nothing in
Italy but the Italian Tyrol. The French troops were also with-

drawn from Rome, and the Italians hope soon to make this ancient city the capital of a re-united Italy.

NORTHERN AND EASTERN EUROPE.

RUSSIA, grown to an overshadowing greatness, entered this century under the rule of the absurd and half-crazed
1801. tyrant, Paul I., who had formed an alliance with Napoleon, and threatened England with war. In March, Paul was assassinated, and his son, Alexander I., a good and amiable prince, ascended the throne.—*Abbott's Russia, pp.* 467–471. *Alexander in Am. Cy,*

England asserting and exercising a right of search of neutral vessels, to prevent their carrying munition of war to France or other hostile countries, Russia, Sweden, and Denmark formed an alliance to resist, by force of arms, any such search. England seized and destroyed the Danish fleet, and Alexander, coming into power, forsook the alliance.—*Gould's Allison, pp.* 148, 149. *Alexander in Am. Cy.*

Alexander was a party to the Third and Fourth Coalitions, and, after the Battle of Jena, advanced to the assistance
1807. of Prussia. Finally, defeated at Friedland, he negotiated with Napoleon the Peace of Tilsit, and formed a strong friendly compact with the French emperor.—*Alexander in Am. Cy. Abbott's Russia, pp.* 483–488.

Bernadotte, a French general, was elected Crown Prince of Sweden, and was adopted by the old king, Charles XIII.,
1810. under the name of Charles John. He at once assumed control of affairs as regent, and, on the death of the king, January, 1812, was crowned as Charles XIV. He soon took sides against Napoleon.—*Bernadotte in Am. Cy.*

Napoleon's measures had again alienated Alexander, and having declared war, he invaded Russia with an immense
1812. force, threatening to destroy the Russian throne. The

events of the campaign have been given under "France."

Russia and Sweden took part in the Grand Coalition, and in the final campaign against Napoleon. Russia was a party to the Holy Alliance.

Greece, long oppressed by the Turks, at length rose in revolt, and began a contest which lasted seven years. Alex-
1821. ander Ypsilanti headed the revolt.—*Modern Eu., Vol.* 3, *p.* 656.

A National Council was assembled, and adopted for Greece a Constitution as an independent government. The Turk-
1822. ish fleet was sent against the island of Scio, and perpetrated massacres of great and terrible enormity.—*Mod. Eu., Vol.* 3, *pp.* 656–657. *Scio in Am. Cy.*

Nicholas I. succeeded his brother, Alexander, on the throne of Russia.—*Abbott's Russia, pp.* 500–504.

1825. The Egyptians, having been called in to assist the Turks, invaded Greece with 14,000.—*Mod. Eu., Vol.* 3, *p.* 658.

Missolonghi, after a siege of more than a year, which attracted the attention of Europe, fell, April 22d, before the com-
1826. bined armies of Turkey and Egypt.—*Missolonghi, Am. Cy.*

The Janizaries, a formidable body of Turkish infantry, having become a terror to the Sultan, were slaughtered to the number of 25,000, and the corps was suppressed.—*Janizaries in Am. Cy.*

The heroic struggle of the Greeks had awakened the sympathy of all civilized nations, and England, France, and
1827. Russia sent a fleet to aid them. By chance, this fleet was drawn into a battle with the Turkish and Egyptian fleet, and destroyed it.—*Mod. Eu., Vol.* 3, *pp.* 658–659.

In May, Russia declared war against Turkey, and sent a large army which took possession of the left bank of the Dan-
1828. ube, and overran Bulgaria.—*Abbott's Russia, p.* 512.

By the treaty of Adrianople, which closed the war with Turkey, Turkey made important concessions to Russia.—
1829. *Abbott's Russia, p.* 513. *Nicholas in Am. Cy.*

In July, the Poles arose in a general insurrection to shake off the Russian yoke. The insurrection was speedily sup-
1830. pressed, and thousands of Poles were banished to

Siberia.—*Abbott's Russia, p.* 513. *Poland in American Cy.*

Greek independence being won, a young Bavarian prince was
chosen as king of Greece, under the title of Otho I.—
1832. *Greece in Am. Cy.*

The evident efforts of Russia to gain control of Turkey, roused
the jealousy of the western powers, and England, France,
1854. and Sardinia took sides with Turkey. The war which
followed, known as the Crimean War, has already been noticed under "England" and "France."

Nicholas, dying during the war, was succeeded by his son,
Alexander II., the reigning monarch.—*Nicholas in*
1855. *Am. Cy.*

By a decree of the emperor, serfdom ceased in Russia, March
3d. This event marks very clearly the mighty progress
1863. Russia has made in civilization during this century.—
Russia in Annual Cy., 1863.

The war between Denmark, and Austria and Prussia stripped
Denmark of a large part of its territories, and left her
1864. with but limited power.—*Schleswig Holstein in Annual*
Cy., 1864.

www.ingramcontent.com/pod-product-compliance
Lightning Source LLC
LaVergne TN
LVHW011223110826
845150LV00006B/1531